ENGLISH DRAMATISTS

Series Editor:
Bruce King

ENGLISH DRAMATISTS
Series Editor: Bruce King

Published titles

Richard Cave, *Ben Jonson*
Christine Richardson and Jackie Johnston, *Medieval Drama*

Forthcoming titles

Susan Bassnett, *Shakespeare: Elizabethan Plays*
Laura Bromley, *Webster and Ford*
John Bull, *Vanbrugh and Farquarson*
Philip McGuire, *Shakespeare: Jacobean Plays*
Kate McKluskie, *Dekker and Heywood*
Max Novak, *Fielding and Gay*
Roger Sales, *Christopher Marlowe*
David Thomas, *William Congreve*
Cheryl Turner, *Early Women Dramatists*
Albert Wertheim, *Etheridge and Wycherley*
Martin White, *Middleton and Tourneur*
Katharine Worth, *Sheridan and Goldsmith*

ENGLISH DRAMATISTS

BEN JONSON

Richard Allen Cave
*Professor of Drama and Theatre Arts in the University of London
at Royal Holloway and Bedford New College*

St. Martin's Press   New York

All rights reserved. For information write:
Scholarly and Reference Division,
St. Martin's Press, Inc., 175 Fifth Avenue,
New York, N.Y. 10010

First published in the United States of America in 1991

Printed in Hong Kong

ISBN 0–312–04250–7

Library of Congress Cataloging-in-Publication Data
Cave, Richard Allen.
Ben Jonson/Richard Allen Cave.
    p.   cm.—(English dramatists)
Includes bibliographical references.
ISBN 0–312–04250–7
1. Jonson, Ben, 1573?–1637—Criticism and interpretation.
I. Title.   II. Series: English dramatists (St. Martin's Press)
PR2638.C35   1990
822′.3—dc20   89–49351
                                                            CIP

Contents

For
Eleanor and Judith

Editor's Preface

Each generation needs to be introduced to the culture and great works of the past and to reinterpret them in its own ways. This series re-examines the important English dramatists of earlier centuries in the light of new information, new interests and new attitudes. The books are written for students, theatre-goers and general readers who want an up-to-date view of the plays and dramatists, with emphasis on drama as theatre and on stage, social and political history. Attention is given to what is known about performance, acting styles, changing interpretations, the stages and theatres of the time and theatre economics. The books will be relevant to those interested in or studying literature, theatre and cultural history.

BRUCE KING

Acknowledgements

The research that has grown into the present volume began some years ago as a consequence of an invitation from Margaret Cottier of the Department of Extra Mural Studies in the University of London: she kindly asked me to take a group of actors and hold two workshops on Jonson, concentrating on a play of my choice, for a Tutors' Residential Specialist Course on Drama that she was running. I chose *Bartholomew Fair* and took four actors – Anne Watkins, John Kennett, Hilary Burr and Gerard Moran: two were professionals, two student-actors with some considerable experience of working under my direction. My aim was to explore some ideas about the relation between actor and audience in Jonson's theatre; we had a highly responsive audience ourselves and the actors accordingly were inspired and inspiring. I am deeply grateful to everyone involved that day and to several generations of final-year students in the Department of Drama and Theatre Studies at Royal Holloway and Bedford New College with whom I have subsequently explored Jonson's plays in seminar and workshop: they have taught me much and helped strengthen the line of argument I had begun to pursue. Bruce King then offered me a choice of dramatist to write on for his new series and the opportunity was forthcoming to marshal the material into a cogent form.

It is not perhaps customary with academic publications to acknowledge a debt to theatre practitioners; but my subject is essentially Jonson's comedies in performance and I would like to express my thanks to several directors who have contributed notably to my appreciation of Jonson's art: Trevor Nunn (*The Alchemist*); Bill Alexander (*Volpone*); Peter Barnes (*Bartholomew Fair* and *The Devil Is An Ass*); Richard Eyre (*Bartholomew Fair*); John Caird (*Every Man In His Humour* and *The New Inn*).

The staff of numerous institutions have helped my research at various stages to run smoothly: I would particularly wish to mention the Press/Publicity and Scripts Departments at the National Theatre; the Library of the Shakespeare Centre at Stratford-upon-Avon; the Library at the Victoria and Albert Museum; and the Study Room at the Theatre Museum. Enid Foster at the British Theatre Association and David Ward of the Library at Royal Holloway and Bedford New College have both given prompt and accurate advice; Brenda Townend and Jo Wootton typed large portions of the manuscript; Michael Leslie generously took time away from his own research to read and comment constructively on the book in typescript; and my wife has been a creative presence at all stages of the volume's progress. I am profoundly indebted to them all.

RAC

1
On Inductions

The prologue to Jonson's last play, *The Sad Shepherd*, opens with a characteristic flourish. There is a reminder of the dramatist's forty-year-long career in the theatre fitting 'fables for your finer ears'. Then comes what at first sounds like a humble apology until the phrasing takes an unexpected turn:

> Although at first he scarce could hit the bore,
> Yet you, with patience harkening more and more,
> At length have grown up to him . . .

It is a skilfully delivered, back-handed compliment; elderly theatre-goers aware of the development of Jonson's career over three reigns and of the range of styles of comedy that he had mastered would have been amused at this witty insistence on one abiding feature in his work: his provocative attitude to audiences, demanding that they cease to hanker after the conventional and bring to an engagement with his plays a wholly open mind. As the prologue continues, Jonson builds on this initial strategy of surprise: we are informed that the play is in the pastoral tradition and are introduced to the main character, the sad shepherd, who 'passeth silently over the stage' mourning his 'lost love', whom he supposes drowned. That would seem to have completed the Prologue's customary business and, with a final couplet expressing hope that the play pleases, he leaves the stage – only to bounce back in immediately with a far less ingratiating tone to justify Jonson's decision to mix

1

pastoral with mirth in the ensuing action. This is not, we are told, a failure in decorum: a play should establish its own unique criteria for judgement.

What is fascinating about all this is that *The Sad Shepherd* is unfinished (only three acts were completed by the time of Jonson's death) and yet the prologue, which many a dramatist might have left to be a routine final effort, has been conceived already as an essential part of the exposition. 'Strategy' would seem the operative word here, since Jonson is cunningly and decisively preparing his audience's frame of mind and giving them at the outset a perspective on the play by deliberately making them conscious of themselves as spectators, experienced playgoers familiar with his own past work and the corpus of contemporary British drama within which he has striven to make a distinctive contribution. The idea of a *relaxed* audience would seem to have been anathema to Jonson, since 'relaxed' could easily mean 'apathetic'. This is in part the result of the strong didactic impulse behind his work: Jonson saw comedy as a markedly serious as well as a hilarious business. The need to find and sustain a sensitive balance where laughter was an expression of a deepening awareness was the stimulus to his creating a wealth of strategies to keep his audiences alert to their responsibilities at a performance. Jonson's initial tactic is frequently to remind an audience precisely where it is and why: looking at a stage where certain gifted individuals are cleverly transforming themselves with our connivance in order to execute a work of imaginative artifice that he has troubled to devise. His inductions are in consequence firmly rooted in the here and now on a given stage (and tell us today a great deal about what it was actually like to go to the theatre in Elizabethan, Jacobean or Caroline London). Repeatedly we are made aware that we are engaged in the experience of drama in performance.

Consider an early play, *Cynthia's Revels*. At the moment when we expect formal action we get a trio of the younger boy players squabbling over who will speak the prologue. It is not only childish, it is highly unprofessional conduct in front of a paying audience. (The play that follows is to be about courtiers who consider that their position gives them the right to behave irresponsibly.) The lads decide to draw lots; the most demonstrative of the three still fails to get the chance to hold the stage, so he decides to hog it forcibly and, out of spite since Jonson did not choose him as prologue in the first place, to recount the plot so as to rob the play of all element of surprise. This proves no easy task: the other boys repeatedly try to gag him, while he becomes increasingly staggered by the complications of the intrigue he is trying to summarise. (Plot in *Cynthia's Revels* will soon prove of less importance than the depiction of character.) Determined to ruin the performance somehow, he next seizes the cloak traditionally worn by speakers of prologues, swathes it about him and begins to mimic the more eccentric kinds of playgoer: first the man whose pedestrian deliberations are punctuated by long puffs at his pipe and then the 'better-gather'd gallant' who draws attention to his fine clothes by ostentatiously calling for the author or loudly criticising the stale wit of most modern plays. (Caricature will be the main business of the play.) Suddenly, as if conscious of a change in the quality of the laughter being provoked, the three companions sidle away, troubled lest they have gone too far and offended their audience. Finally the prologue-elect gets his chance to speak: his words are an appeal to all discerning persons present and an assertion that Jonson's muse 'shuns the print of any beaten path'.

We seem to have been given, impromptu, a view of the precarious and tense life back-stage, all that normally lies unseen behind the ordered artifice on-stage. In time we will find this reflects subtly on the issues and dramatic method of the play that follows; more importantly it reflects on actor–audience relations in a fashion calculated to leave the actual audience bemused as to what is expected of it as a proper response. The illusion of a haphazard, improvised quality about this opening suggests by force of contrast that choices and a scrupulous exercise of judgement have gone to the shaping of the ensuing action which the dramatist expects his audience to come to terms with and respect. The induction exposes to an audience what one might term the mechanics of performance. Judgement is expressed, literally, as a taking of stances, role-play and assumptions of character. Even off-stage and apparently unscripted as here, the players never stop *acting*, or so we are led to suppose; seemingly they make any place a playing-space.

In general Jonson's inductions similarly disconcert by blurring the distinctions between life and the arts of the theatre. *Every Man Out Of His Humour*, for example, has Asper, the supposed author of the piece, seat two friends on-stage and explain to them the theory of humours which his play explores; he leaves and, as nothing seems to be happening, the friends while away the time with a discussion about tradition and the individual talent in respect of the writing of comedy. When the prologue finally enters, one of the friends jokingly says that, if a performer had not appeared soon, he would have spoken the prologue himself; the choleric actor takes him at his word and promptly leaves him the stage. Cordatus' tongue-tied embarrassment is relieved by the arrival of one of the *characters* from the play, Buffone, who, deep in his cups, toasts the audience, reminisces about dining and wining with Jonson and boasts that no dramatist, however strong his didactic intent, will ever improve his personal disposition or habits. We are being deliberately confused as to which dimension of reality we are in at any point here. Asper the dramatist is to appear in the play as Macilente, but it is a role in the action that the dramatist clearly plays under another name in life. The two friends are ostensibly just spectators, yet they are sharply characterised by the nature of their critical judgements. When the genial Buffone talks of Jonson, is he speaking as actor or as character? Significantly the only plays by Jonson that do not carry Inductions or dramatised Prologues like this are ones such as *Volpone*, *Epicoene*, *The Alchemist* or *The New Inn* where the immediate business of the first act involves role-play, impersonation, dressing-up, the creating of scenarios for private sport and the deliberate choice to act as audience of another's activity, incidents in which the mechanics of performance are again laid bare before us.

Recent criticism of Renaissance drama has made much of its meta-theatrical nature, that built-in awareness within a play that it is a theatrical construct. As Lionel Abel,[1] one of the pioneers of this approach, expressed it, these are 'theatre-pieces about life seen as already theatricalised', in which characters 'are aware of their own theatricality'. 'None of us,' he argues, 'knows the form of the plot that he is in, and Hamlet was the first theatrical figure who expressed this fact fully.' Shakespeare and Calderon are usually cited as the most sophisticated exponents of meta-theatre, but Jonson's great comedies too show the ubiquity in the fabric of life of *performance*, whether it is consciously or innocently undertaken. One of the finest of his last plays shows a character (Lovel) actually troubled to desperation by the fact of that ubiquity.

Where Jonson differs from Shakespeare is in devising strategies continually to implicate his audience in that awareness. He exploits all the devices that constitute the art of performance until performance comes to have the flexibility of reference (philosophical, emotional and social) of a metaphysical conceit. Jonson's is a wholly purposeful theatricality, as his witty Inductions suggest, exacting in its demands on spectators but richly rewarding for those who comply. His plays have not been as well served by the modern theatre as have Shakespeare's, Marlowe's, even Webster's, which is surprising, given his concern with creating an 'alienated' audience, one made conscious (as Brecht would have his spectators) of participating in the shaping of an artifice the better to perceive the imaginative consequences signified by the performance. It is often said by contemporary practitioners that his plays are difficult of access, and yet Jonson is the most flamboyantly theatrical of Renaissance dramatists. The most successful of recent productions have been ones which clearly began in rehearsal by investigating theatricality as the vehicle which would best convey an audience into an imaginative engagement with Jonson's themes. That is similarly to be the strategy adopted by this study.

It would be wrong to suppose from this that Jonson's approach to playwriting was exclusively cerebral. He was a gifted intellectual, certainly; and proud of the fact of being educated (despite his step-father's lowly status as a bricklayer) at Westminster School under William Camden; his command of classical literature was formidable, as a glance at the annotations to *Sejanus* or to a masque such as *Hymenaei* will confirm; his knowledge of contemporary literature and drama was as wide-ranging; and he was an intimate of the households of many of the notable scholars and learned aristocrats of his day. There was no great malice, given Jonson's personal accomplishments, in his describing his friend and colleague, Shakespeare, as having little Latin and less Greek. But Jonson's remarkable erudition was offset by as prodigious an appetite for life and a great relish for the absurd, quixotic and outrageous in human behaviour. His own experience encompassed extremes: he underwent the hazards of being a soldier in Flanders and an itinerant actor before he fully established a career in literature and theatre; though Jonson was three times imprisoned (for his part in the authorship and performance of *The*

Isle of Dogs (1597) which was considered seditious; for the killing in a duel of a fellow-actor in Henslowe's company (1598) when he only escaped hanging by pleading benefit of clergy; and for his collaboration with Chapman and Marston in *Eastward Ho!* (1605) which was deemed satirical at the king's expense) and was under suspicion of a peripheral involvement in the Gunpowder Plot of 1605, he gained the favour of King James. Despite his illustrious friends and patrons and the quite considerable sums of money assigned him once he began regularly devising entertainments for the Stuart Court, he was frequently in want and died in a state of near-poverty. A carefully edited Folio of his Collected Plays (1616) published by William Stansby courageously broke new cultural ground in assuming that modern – as distinct from classical – drama had literary as well as theatrical merit and that the best of such work was not of ephemeral but of enduring value – an action and attitude that clearly inspired Heminges and Condell to secure Shakespeare's work for posterity seven years later. Yet all but two of the works contained in the Folio are comedies or farces attacking his fellow men for being the dupes of their own folly, madness and untutored imagination. The plays teem with hare-brained schemes, ludicrous posturings, preposterous (though accurately observed) jargon, grandiose rhetoric, wild knockabout and accelerating frantic action of a breaktaking ingenuity of invention. There is a precarious sense with most of the comedies that the characters have such dynamism that they will evade Jonson's artistic control. The excitement of the plays in performance comes from a constant tension between extremes: on the one hand a cleverly sustained illusion that all we watch is freewheeling and spontaneous, on the other an equally carefully sustained logic of development and motivation. Each of Jonson's Jacobean comedies is a daring flight of the imagination yet, classicist that he was, he always aims the flight at a specific objective, however surprising, wayward or seemingly haphazard the course to it.

Comedy proved more Jonson's *métier* than tragedy; but within the one genre he excelled in an array of different styles. Several possible reasons for this suggest themselves. Unlike Shakespeare, who wrote exclusively for adult acting-troupes and for much of his career exclusively for one company (the Lord Chamberlain's, subsequently the King's Men), Jonson tackled the whole range of playing spaces and types of companies available to the Elizabethan and Stuart dramatist. While most of his major plays were acted by the King's Men at the Globe or, after 1610, at the Blackfriars Theatre, he did prentice work for Henslowe and wrote a substantial number of comedies for one of the troupes of boy-actors (the Children of the Chapel Royal, subsequently the Children of the Queen's Revels playing at Blackfriars) which demanded a completely different approach to characterisation, tone, verbal artistry. Far from being daunted by the need to work within the limitations of such players, Jonson proved immensely versatile in his offerings, which extend from pastiche of Plautus in *The Case Is Altered* through the dramatic satire of *The Poetaster* to the comedy of manners and sexual mores in *Epicoene*, which Emrys Jones has aptly dubbed 'the first West End comedy'. *Bartholomew Fair* was presented by Lady Elizabeth's Men at the recently opened Hope Theatre on Bankside in 1614 prior to a staging at the Palace of Whitehall, while Jonson's last performed work, *The Tale of a Tub* (1633) was mounted by Queen Henrietta's Men at the Cockpit, the select indoor theatre in Drury Lane. In addition to working for all the available kinds of public theatres, Jonson also from 1605–31 devised with Inigo Jones a series of spectacular court masques for private performance chiefly at Whitehall. Within a short space of time he was adapting the form of dramatised panegyric he originally created for these to accommodate a wealth of comic material, yet even here the flight into fantastic and whimsical humour was always harnessed to a specific rhetorical, political, and in time metaphysical, purpose.

A second possible reason for Jonson's command of a rich multiplicity of styles lies in his responsiveness to changing fashions in theatrical taste. He was decidedly a man *of* his age (or rather ages, given the length of his creative life) yet of sufficiently detached an integrity to be at all times one of its shrewdest critics. His involvement in the 'War of the Theatres' is a manifest example of what was generally a subtler tendency in his art. Between 1599 and 1602 Jonson (writing for the Children of the Chapel Royal and the King's Men) did battle with Marston and Dekker (working for the Children of Paul's); they composed plays ridiculing each other's style, attitude and personality. Doubtless the whole affair made for excellent publicity and good takings for the rival companies of boy-actors, but behind Jonson's involvement one can presume a more searching intent, given the tenor of the rest of his work. Marston he satirised for his egocentric mannerisms and abuse of language, Dekker for his doggedly pathetic conventionalism. From his first extant play to his last incomplete one Jonson shows himself suspicious of the popular and the conventional as too easygoing imaginatively and often too lax morally. It became a recurring feature of his dramatic artistry to deconstruct fashionable styles of comedy so as to expose the dubious social and moral assumptions that lay behind their formulaic patterning. It was a satirical impulse of this kind that habitually triggered Jonson's creativity, enabling him to innovate and develop a wholly personal mode of city comedy in his middle years and an original style of romantic comedy in the Caroline age in reaction against the excursions by Charles's court into neo-Platonic pastoral, like Walter Montague's *The Shepherd's Paradise*. The canon of Jonson's comedies is in many ways a guide to the development of the theatre in England from the 1590s until his death in 1637 as reflected in the sensibility of a man who was at once acutely responsive to the immediate tenor of the times yet of a sufficiently robust intelligence never to become the times' minion.

This brings us back again to Jonson's audiences, since his dramatic strategies are clearly directed at inspiring a similarly attentive detachment in them, which is why a thorough imaginative engagement with those strategies during a performance of a Jonsonian comedy can be an inspiring and exhilarating experience. Jonson was an intellectual and he made the play of the intellect central to an audience's experience of his comedies; he was also (in the fullest and best sense) a complete man of the theatre who knew the precise value of theatricality when it was both potent and scrupulously directed.

2
Elizabethan Jonson

Jonson's earliest extant play, *The Case Is Altered*,[1] was popular enough to merit revivals, revision and up-dating of the satirical content, and publication in a Quarto, though the dramatist himself chose not to include it in the Folio of 1616. There are several possible reasons for this. It is the closest Jonson came – to judge by the surviving plays – to writing in the spirit of the typical Elizabethan comedy with its delight in densely-packed action, wondrous event and an array of reunions and marriages to make for a harmonious conclusion – a form of drama that Jonson was later to criticise and repudiate as escapist, lacking in realism. Then there was the fact that at least one contemporary, Fitzgeoffrey, judged the play as outright plagiarism of Plautus.[2] Finally there is the satirical material (deemed to have been added when the play was acquired by the child-actors at Blackfriars around 1600) which attacks theatre-audiences as oafish, ill-discerning, unwilling to engage imaginatively with original work: the implication is that *The Case Is Altered* achieved popularity in spite of itself, that the stubbornly sentimental Elizabethan public saw in it what they wanted to see (which in some measure they were conditioned to do by prevailing conventions of comedy) and not what Jonson wished them to see. They missed the satire and burlesque. It was not the last time in Jonson's career that playwright and audience were to be at cross-purposes.

Let us consider the charge of plagiarism. The play is consciously derived from Plautus' *The Pot of Gold (Aulularia)* and *The*

Prisoners (Captivi) but this was not uncommon practice in the period as Shakespeare's *Comedy of Errors*, based on the *Menaechmi*, shows. What is remarkable in Jonson's case is that he has borrowed the intricate plot-structures of *two* comedies and with considerable ingenuity interwoven them to create the sense of a teeming social life on stage. To complicate the intrigue further he has given the miser's daughter, Rachel, not two suitors as in Plautus but five, thereby producing a range of potential rivalries: between father and son, friend and friend, master and man. By uniting two complex plots Jonson includes just about every kind of romantic 'marvel' which New Comedy favoured to secure a happy ending: no fewer than three 'lost' children are recovered (two sons by Fernese and a sister by Chamont); a poor girl (Rachel) is found to be an aristocrat, while a manservant (Gasper) is in truth a Count's heir; both these seemingly lowly characters are sensed by certain choice nobles to have marks of distinctive breeding about them long before their actual identities and status are discovered; the miser is united with his stolen treasure, the heroine is saved from possible rape by the fortuitous return of her long-absent lover and a treacherous friend is discovered for what he is but is forgiven. Jonson's organisation of these multiple surprises is nothing short of brilliant but, as there are so many, the effect is somewhat mechanical (all this intricate catastrophe is achieved in the space of two scenes and some 340 lines of text). The fact that the action is punctuated with joyous litanies such as 'O my son, my son!' – 'My dearest Rachel!' – 'My most honey gold' ensures the tone is closer to the farcical than the miraculous (V. iv. p. 715). From the first, New Comedy sustained a healthy scepticism about the improbability of its plot-devices: Menander, Plautus and Terence in diverse ways all tease their audiences with a sense of the absurdity of theatrical artifice for which they are willing to suspend their disbelief. Elizabethan romantic comedy employed these same devices but took them seriously, even, in Shakespeare's case, endowing them with an increasingly rich psychological verisimilitude. Was the classicist in Jonson trying in *The Case Is Altered* to restore a necessary balance and purge Elizabethan audiences of their tendency to sentimental indulgence? If those audiences relished complex plots and romantic resolutions, then he would give them intrigue and romance in such abundance that the utter improbability of it all would be obvious; in laughing at the sheer artifice, the audience would be laughing at their own susceptibilities and their desire for a theatre offering emotional consolations. Delusions, especially sentimental ones, are, however, not easily or radically shifted; and one cannot but wonder whether, if this were Jonson's strategy with *The Case Is Altered*, audiences were so inured to convention that they accepted the play at face-value and wantonly missed its satirical perspective. The evidence, especially the later insertions castigating audiences as mindless and apathetic, would suggest that this was what happened.[3] Interestingly, several of Jonson's ensuing plays were to include devices that quite dogmatically instruct audiences *how* to respond to the comedy, while the absolute intransigence of people in the grip of delusions was in time to be the subject of much of Jonson's funniest work. It is a lucky chance that *The Case Is Altered* has survived, for it usefully indicates some of Jonson's early thinking about audience reactions; that the critical strategy adopted there appears to have failed helps to explain why he began to explore increasingly sophisticated devices to make an audience conscious both of its relation to the stage and of the artifice involved in the art of acting. His future plays steadily and relentlessly anatomise the experience that we call theatre.

It would be wrong to suggest that *The Case Is Altered* is concerned purely with burlesque, strong though that element is. Since the art and criticism of T.S. Eliot we have become alert to the possibilities of creative allusion, of the witty quotation or misquotation of authors from the past as a means of highlighting a significant shift in moral, social or cultural values between that past and the present. This has always been an in-built part of the tradition of New Comedy; Plautus and Terence were conscious of their precise debts to Menander and Menander seemingly of his to the later work of Euripides. The tradition was called to mind the better to define the precise originality, the *difference* of the current work. Jonson similarly seems to be deliberately reminding his audience of the tradition by extensively 'quoting' from Plautus to draw attention to where *The Case Is Altered* differs markedly from the two Roman comedies on which it is based; moreover the very preposterousness of the Plautine material serves to invest these new elements with a vivid immediacy. The low-life scenes in the servants' hall, which are written in a very different vein from scenes involving wily slaves in classical comedy, root the play in the believable world of a Renaissance court rather than the never-never-land in which *Aulularia* and *Captivi* take place. The debate between Fernese's daughters, Aurelia and Phoenixella, about the advantages of cultivating detachment in the face of life's pleasures and adversities provides a welcome corrective to the emotional extremes experienced by the characters more directly involved in the complexities of the action. Most important of all is Jonson's handling of the central figure in each of his two plots, the miser, Jaques, and the distressed father, Fernese, who have greater psychological complexity than their prototypes in Plautus, Euclio and Hegio. Whereas Plautus preserves a wry objectivity, seeing his characters as an occasion for farce and for diverse patterns of comic misunderstanding, Jonson characteristically offers (and invites) imaginative engagement with the obsessions that propel his. In consequence Jonson's two characters seem larger than the play-world they inhabit and constantly threaten to break out of the bounds of the conventions imposed by that form of comedy. Surrounded by a deliberately over-worked and conscious artifice, Jaques and Fernese seem disturbingly *real*.

There are some significant differences in plotting. Where Euclio, a poor man, has found by chance the hoard of gold that he strives to hide, Jacques, formerly a respected steward in a great household, has stolen his wealth and his master's daughter, Rachel, and assumed the disguise of a poor man to keep his true identity secret; he must hoard the gold since spending it would be to risk detection. Because he can lead no viable public life, Jaques has let gold occupy the place of all social relations and all values in his consciousness; digging a new hole in which to bury his treasure, he addresses it fondly: 'In, my dear life! sleep sweetly, my dear child!' (III. ii. p. 692). At other times he calls the money his good 'angels' and 'beauteous ghost'. The terms here are crucial for they serve to link Jaques in the audience's mind with Fernese, a genuine father who is haunted by the 'beauteous ghost' of a lost son, Camillo, and who in consequence is intensely possessive of his remaining son, Paulo. In *Captivi* Plautus begins his play near the climax of Hegio's story when his son is already being held a prisoner of war in Elis and Hegio himself has acquired two enemy prisoners in order to put into operation a plan to redeem his beloved Philopolemus. Jonson begins his plot long before the outbreak of hostilities between Milan and France in which Paulo will be captured. This allows him to devote considerable stage-time to showing the precise effect on Fernese of the loss of Camillo when a child (during a previous battle with the French in which the Count's home was sacked). Fernese constantly sends servants racing through home and gardens (we hear their voices calling from every angle of the stage) to search Paulo out the moment his absence from the Count's chamber is noted; Paulo has to be devious to gain a moment's privacy. When war with France is imminent, Fernese makes the commander, Maximilian, swear never to take his eyes off Paulo during the campaign and to plan for nothing but Paulo's safety. This is as comic as Jaques' fussing over his gold and repeatedly running off stage at the slightest sound to check that no one has discovered its whereabouts – comic, but not harshly so; it is not ridiculous, for the psychological motivation is in each case wholly understandable. Both men are seen to be powerfully subject to the workings of guilt, the one for a tangible crime, the other (more subtly) for a sense of failure in his parental responsibilities. Obsession in them runs much deeper than eccentricity.

In his two comedies Plautus offers a prologue which implies that all the complex intrigue will have a happy outcome: the gold, we discover, has been placed in Euclio's way deliberately by the household god to enable the old man to give his daughter a handsome dowry; and we learn that one of the prisoners Hegio has acquired is none other than his long lost son, Tyndarus. The information allows us to sit detached, bemused, superior to Euclio and Hegio and view them as the dupes of chance. With Jonson's comedy we stand in a very different relation to the characters: Jaques announces his personal guilt in a soliloquy on his first appearance in the action; and, though we may suspect young Gasper is the lost son, Camillo, the fact is not confirmed for us until the moment that Fernese himself discovers it. Throughout we experience the characters on their own terms and so, as the stage-action involving them grows more intricate, we can appreciate how its effect on them is to intensify their private obsessions. Euclio and Hegio never pose a serious threat to the world of the plays they inhabit; Jaques and Fernese do. The Machiavellian Angelo, one of Rachel's many suitors, decides to defeat the others by exploiting Jaques' mania for gold; under cover of darkness he has a servant sing out Jaques' name and when the miser appears places gold coins ('angels') at intervals in his path, thereby luring him away from the house. Jaques is in ecstasies: the sound of the falling gold is like the music of the spheres. It is a wonderfully conceived scene showing how Jaques has utterly lost touch with reality and his proper responsibilities. He should be guarding Rachel's honour but, even as he is seduced forth by the apparent shower of gold, Rachel is being abducted by Angelo who, once he has her alone, threatens rape. Our laughter quickly gravitates to a more complex response. The situation with Fernese grows even darker than this. Paulo is captured by the French and Lord Chamont and his friend Gasper by Maximilian; Fernese readily agrees that Gaspar should be sent as ambassador to the French to secure an exchange of the two most prized prisoners, Paulo for Chamont. When the Count discovers that Chamont and Gasper assumed each other's identity on being captured and that in consequence the *actual* Lord Chamont has gone home a freed man, he is beside himself with rage; he refuses to recognise, for all Gasper and Maximilian's careful reasoning, that trust and affection can exist in any relationship except that of father and son. He threatens Gasper with death if Chamont fails to return with Paulo by the agreed time and, when that eventuality occurs and the court refuse to carry out his orders, prepares to execute Gasper himself. He would do violence (as events quickly prove) on the very son whose loss is the root of his obsession. Romantic conventions intervene to save both situations: miraculously in the nick of time, Paulo appears to protect Rachel and a sudden vision of his lost child Camillo stays Fernese's hand. Both strands of plot have come perilously close to tragedy to a degree never permitted in Plautine comedy, an effect that is enhanced by the sheer preposterousness of the devices whereby the tragic outcome is averted. Jaques and Fernese have become dangerous figures in the play-world because no one in that world takes their obsessions seriously. And that – in a fashion that will become increasingly characteristic of Jonson – is to pose the audience a challenge and make them question the grounds on which they have been laughing at these two characters. Jonson refuses to let his audience sit smugly superior to the play in performance.

The Case Is Altered is clearly prentice work; but in the portrayal of Jaques and Fernese and in the strategies designed to jolt an audience into a criticial awareness of their tendency to adopt a passive or sentimental relation to the stage-action, we can detect qualities and techniques that anticipate many of the strengths of Jonson's great Jacobean comedies. The evidence, as we have seen, suggests that audiences liked the play for the wrong reasons; a proper appreciation of its best effects does require a sound knowledge of Plautus, which not all members of Jonson's audience would have at their command. In his four remaining Elizabethan comedies Jonson chose to step up the attack on his audiences' susceptibilities and to increase the consciously aesthetic and intellectual content. In consequence the didactic approach, always strong in Jonson, began to veer closer and closer to dogmatism: he would compel the audience to acknowledge that in his hands comedy was a serious business. *Every Man Out of His Humour*,[4] for example, announces its intention immediately: here come 'pills to purge' the follies of the time; 'deformity', we are promised, will be 'anatomised in every nerve and sinew'. (Induction, pp. 63–4). Then for the audience follows a severe challenge:

> *Good men, and virtuous spirits*, that loath their vices,
> Will cherish my free labours, love my lines.
>
> (Induction, p. 63)

Where *The Case Is Altered* overdid the plotting for satirical ends, *Every Man In His Humour, Every Man Out of His Humour, Cynthia's Revels* and *The Poetaster* increasingly abandon plot in the traditional sense in preference for a sequence of telling incidents in which one by one all but a handful of 'select' characters are exposed as fools, asses, dolts and zanies. The middle and upper classes (merchants, landed gentry, lawyers, students, courtiers) are shown to be obsessed with trivialities and a prey to affectation, and so the world they create about themselves is inevitably a cultural, moral and spiritual void. The two later plays were composed for performance by boy-actors (the Children of the Chapel Royal playing at Blackfriars) whose short stature and piping voices must have made the characters' self-importance seem even more preposterous. The very conditions of performance became part of Jonson's process of cutting gross egocentricity down to its proper size: the characters are ignoring the responsibilities of adulthood and behaving childishly.

Lest audiences should feel rebellious against this new style of comedy, Jonson began to include instruction on how best to respond to his work. First with *Every Man Out of His Humour* he borrowed a device from Kyd's *The Spanish Tragedy* (Jonson had apparently played the role of Hieronymo early in his career as an actor and he wrote additional scenes at Henslowe's request for a later revival[5]) where two characters sit on-stage as an extension of the audience and comment on the progress of the action. In Kyd this works as a means of providing and maintaining tension and suspense: the two characters are the ghost of a murdered knight (Don Andrea) and a personification of Revenge who is sent from Hades to satisfy the ghost with a show of how his assassins themselves meet with a gruesome death. In Jonson's comedy the two characters who frame the action, and offer a commentary on it, Cordatus and Mitis, are critics and intellectuals. Cordatus is the more assertive figure who patiently educates his companion to appreciate the play's finer points, its relation to the history of the genre and to various classical prescriptions about what makes for the ideal comedy. Mitis accepts it all meekly. Once he does voice the suggestion that a good, old-fashioned love-story with plenty of intrigue (rather, we suppose, in Shakespeare's manner) would be more to his taste but he is severely rebuked (III. i. p. 105). It could be suggested that Jonson is stacking the cards too heavily in his own favour by putting the defence of conventional Elizabethan comedy in the mouth of someone so completely submissive, but one has to admire Jonson's courage at the end when the supposed actor-author of the play we have watched, Asper, steps out of his role as Macilente and asks the two critics, 'Gentlemen, how like you it? Has't not been *tedious*?' Cordatus replies with superb tact: 'Nay, we have done censuring now' (V. vii. p. 145). One can but wonder how the actual audience responded!

It would be unjust to Jonson to answer Asper's question with a loud affirmative. The play is far from tedious, but there are long stretches of it that are resolutely *undramatic*. Part of the problem is that the satire, unlike that in *The Alchemist* or *Bartholomew Fair*, or interestingly even its companion-piece *Every Man In His Humour*, is spread over too wide a range of targets to the point where the play loses thematic focus: it wants some clearly defined principle of organisation. Time and again the characters severally shed their individuality and step outside the action to comment like chorus-figures on the other people present on stage. They tell us *how* to view and judge. The expositions are skilfully done and generally very witty but they considerably restrict an audience's freedom of response. We repeatedly are offered *statement* when what we want is a dramatic *rendering* of the characters' quirky temperaments. Occasionally Jonson changes his method and we get a glimpse of a more imaginative portrayal of eccentricity: nothing that Macilente says, for example, in introducing the miser Sordido to us provokes as much laughter as Sordido's own soliloquy in which he plans to bury his great stores of corn and disguise his haystacks by covering them with straw and chaff so that, when the bad harvest that he is expecting occurs, he can hold on to his grain and provender until he can sell them at the most advantageous prices. This is character defined through its intimate processes of thought and, in case we should think Sordido merely absurd, Jonson lets our laughter grow through nineteen lines then ends the speech with a couplet that opens our judgement out into wider social and moral implications:

> What though a world of wretches starve the while;
> He that will thrive must think no courses vile. (I. i. p. 75)

This is a dextrous handling of audience-response, powerful for its subtly calculated shock. Macilente told us Sordido was 'a precious, dirty, damned rogue' (I. i. p. 72); now we have *experienced* his viciousness for a fact.

Given our sense of the importance of *Every Man Out of His Humour* in Jonson's development as a necessary if flawed experiment in his quest for a personal style for comedy, we can afford to be charitably disposed towards its special pleading; not all Jonson's contemporaries were inclined to be so generous. Marston and Dekker took issue with Jonson, making him the butt of several dramatised satires; the ever-combative Jonson did not resist the urge to reply in like kind. The main charges against Jonson were that he was motivated by envy, spleen and arrogance; that he diagnosed the shortcomings of others but could see no wrong in himself: rather he had the effrontery to offer a grossly idealised portrait of himself in Asper (the charge was repeated later regarding Crites in *Cynthia's Revels* and Horace in *The Poetaster*) when in truth he was tetchy, shabby, lecherous, vain and, most damning for a writer, pedestrian. The implication was clear: Jonson the moralist was a sham. Jonson's response was partly to turn a brilliant spotlight on to Marston and Dekker's inadequacies and affectations as writers but more importantly he chose to build dramatic situations out of an idea he had voiced briefly in the Induction to *Every Man Out of His Humour*: namely that '*good* men . . . love my lines' (p. 63). In *Cynthia's Revels* the all-seeing, all-knowing goddess elects Crites, the satirical poet and dramatist, to be the arbiter of taste and regulator of morals at her court and in *The Poetaster* the emperor Augustus champions Horace (clearly another of Jonson's *personae*) against his detractors.[6] Both plays set out to demonstrate the quiet confidence that comes to the poet who accepts the burden of his vocation with due decorum and seriousness. The problem is that neither play pitches its poet-hero against a worthy opponent who merits a display of moral anger. Cynthia's courtiers, who are Crites' enemies, are butterfly-minded, idle exquisites who show scant respect for their position, integrity or education, and are so self-absorbed that they are impervious even to Cupid's love-darts, while the poetasters that are Horace's rivals in Rome are more interested in the manner than the matter of their art, style being no more than a means of self-display. Jonson shows considerable invention in keeping such fundamentally dull people continually entertaining, but neither the courtiers nor the poetasters pose a real threat to the moral order of their worlds and they certainly pose none to the spectator's powers of discrimination. Both plays lack the element of danger for an audience which characterises Jonson's comedy at its finest and which began to be reached at moments in *The Case Is Altered* and *Every Man Out of His Humour*. The moral schemes underlying *Cynthia's Revels* and *The Poetaster* are by contrast with *Volpone* or *The Alchemist* too clear-cut, the conclusions too easily achieved.

There is one episode in *The Poetaster* that embraces an element of danger – that is when the young Ovid *stages* an imitation of a banquet of the gods (IV. iii. p. 272ff.) He assigns each of his friends, their lovers or spouses the role of a particular god or goddess to play (the choice is in each case wittily apt), while he impersonates Jupiter and his lover Julia, the emperor's daughter, Hera. Plays-within-plays are invariably engrossing for an audience and this is no exception: it is a delightful conceit and the gaiety of the performers is infectious. Steadily, however, a more sinister tone intrudes as we realise that the play-acting is being used as an excuse by the 'actors' to throw all moral and sexual restraints aside: it is not the gods in their majestic roles as guardians of order in the universe and shapers of destiny that are being imitated, but the gods in their private capacities as beings beyond shame who pursue their lusts with unbridled relish. The 'play' rapidly degenerates into an orgy with Ovid-Jupiter proposing that the company let their drunken imaginations run riot; suddenly the emperor appears and calls the proceedings to an abrupt conclusion, sending Ovid into exile and imprisoning Julia as authors of the outrage and blasphemy. Ovid is a fine poet (the opening scene of the play establishes that fact clearly), but one who betrays his sublime gift of imagination by wasting it in merely gratifying his desires and vanity: he uses his art to indulge his circle and himself in romantic excess. Ovid would have made a worthy opponent to set alongside Horace with his high claims for the social responsibility of poetry. Interestingly, Horace accompanies the emperor when he breaks up the banquet but he is given only one line in the scene and that an appeal for Caesar's clemency. This is the one moment in the play when Ovid and Horace are on stage together, but they are denied any debate about their different claims for the art of poetry; Jonson otherwise presents them through two parallel and alternating lines of plot that never interact in any creative conflict. Why does Horace attempt to speak in Ovid's defence, when Ovid's principles and practice as a poet are wholly opposed to his own, yet sits in elaborate judgement on the manifest scribblers, Demetrius (Dekker) and Crispinus (Marston), who are small fry by comparison? *The Poetaster* seems suddenly to lose a proper sense of direction and decorum, shrinking its focus down to merely personal issues. Though the purging of Crispinus, who is made to vomit forth his tortuously affected vocabulary ('O – *glibbery* – *lubrical* – *defunct* – O – !' V. i. p. 296) is a conception worthy of Aristophanes, the scene lacks the rich complexity of the earlier banquet where Jonson lures his audience through laughter into delighted complicity in the stage-action only to shock them suddenly with an awareness of the exact implications of what they are enjoying so expansively. This is moral satire of a far higher order than the lambasting of Dekker and Marston. Hesitantly Jonson was finding his way forward to a new art of comedy, one

that required of him a deft and subtle handling of audience-
response.

With *Every Man Out of His Humour, Cynthia's Revels* and *The
Poetaster* one often feels that individual episodes have a greater
comic vivacity than the plays overall; this is not, however, a
criticism that could be levelled at *Every Man In His Humour*.[7]
The earliest and the best of the four satirical comedies, it is the
one work of Jonson's from the Elizabethan period that has had a
continuing life on the English stage: Garrick and Kean played
Kitely, Dickens essayed Bobadil, and it proved the ideal choice
as the first non-Shakespearean play to be staged at the newly-
opened Swan Theatre at Stratford. It shares many characteristics
with the group of plays to which it belongs: there is no continuous
plot though the characters create various episodic intrigues (such
as Wellbred's scheme that brings Kitely and his wife, Cash and
old Knowell severally to Cob's house under the suspicion that it is
a brothel where each mistakenly believes the others to be intent
on adultery); much of the action is devoted to exposing to ridicule
a series of fools who are the dupes of contemporary fashions in
clothes or behaviour, of their idle imaginings or their inflated egos;
some thought is given to the proper status and function of the
poet in society; romantic elements are few, pushed firmly into the
background and treated perfunctorily. How then does this play
achieve an organic unity lacking in its counterparts and why has it
sustained an enduring popularity when, like them, its concerns are
very much of reference to its specific time of composition?

It is not often that Jonson (unlike Shakespeare) signals in his
opening scenes to the alert spectator through a careful reiteration
of certain words or images what the inner thematic explorations
of his play are going to be. *Every Man In His Humour* is an
exception: significantly in the space of his first scene the word
'gentleman' occurs 11 times; by the end of Act One the number
has risen to 33 and by the close of the play the usages total more
than 100. (This refers to the Quarto 'Italian' text; in the revised
'English' version of the comedy in the Folio the deployment of
the term over the various acts is marginally different but the overall
total is the same.) As the action evolves, 'gentleman' attracts to
itself words that by analogy or contrast seem to encourage a
sharpening of definitions: 'gentility', 'gentle', 'manhood', 'lineage',
'gallants', 'rake-hells', and 'signior outsides' in the Quarto, and

'fellow', 'rascals', 'creatures' in the Folio. That what distinguishes a gentleman from a rascal is more than a matter of lineage or 'outside' appearances and has much to do with gentility is indeed the play's theme, but it is less schematic in its development, less obvious and heavy-handed than these bare statistics may suggest. For one thing the term 'gentleman' varies in significance according to the context of its use: it may be at its simplest a conventional and polite form of address or a reference to an unknown person's sex or apparent social status; but with certain characters it can through repetition become a means of self-assertion ('as I am a gentleman') that with seemingly casual indifference flaunts a profession of rank and good breeding. Ironically the word comes quicker to the lips of those who are patently not the proper article than of those who are. In *Cynthia's Revels* Crites devises an entertainment for the goddess in which her courtiers appear magnificently masked and attired as personifications of the virtues that bring true distinction to a monarch and her kingdom. When Cynthia wishes to thank the performers she bids them unmask: she and the theatre-audience are confronted by the stark contrast between the beautiful, serene countenances painted on the vizards and the gross, caricature faces of her actual courtiers. There is a huge discrepancy between what they believe themselves to be and what in reality they are. We have watched their idle pursuits, their jealousies, their contests to find the ideal courtly lover and know that they do not cultivate courtliness, gentility and courtesy as states of *mind*. In *Cynthia's Revels* the perspective is wholly satirical; in *Every Man In His Humour* the concern is more with what might constitute a *real* gentleman.

Unlike the three later comedies which are variously situated in a literary conception of ancient Rome, an imaginary 'fustian country' called Gargaphie and (in the case of *Every Man Out of His Humour*) in a strange social void, *Every Man In His Humour* is placed in a precisely ordered society (very definitely London in the revised version). The characters are drawn from a subtly differentiated range of classes and care is taken to define how they come to interrelate: the major roles include a menial worker (Cob, the water-carrier), a family retainer (Brainworm), a reputable city merchant (Kitely) and the trusted cashier of his warehouse (Thomas), a member of the surburban gentry (Knowell), a magistrate (Clement), a seedy man-about-town of no easily recognisable status (Bobadil), and a fishmonger's son desperate to be upwardly mobile (Matthew). Cob is well placed to laugh at Matthew's social pretensions, knowing his family background and upbringing. Though he responds promptly enough to Bobadil's tone of command, Cob has his suspicions of his lodger's airs and graces, not least because necessity compels Bobadil to live at such a humble address. The water-carrier is invariably addressed as 'honest Cob' (the word carries no irony in Jonson's usage as it frequently does in Shakespeare's) and he is indeed frank, speaking his mind fearlessly; though he knows and is angry that his wife lends Bobadil money, often pawning her own things to do so, he never harbours the least suspicion that Tib could be offering Bobadil sexual favours too. Cob may comment on others but his judgements are confined to what he observes or knows as fact. There is a fine contrast here with the newly-wed Kitely: he knows of no facts whatsoever that might in any way compromise his wife's good name yet his rampant imagination is continually conjuring up visions of himself as a cuckold on the slightest of pretexts. Another point of contrast with Cob is Brainworm: as the manservant in a large household, his security depends on pleasing his social superiors; knowing how to stay in their good favour requires him to judge them and their temperaments shrewdly; he has the facelessness of the born servant because he is immensely adaptable, having the ability to play in his person diverse roles as occasion demands. (Brainworm is a brilliant development of the wily slave of Roman comedy.) The roles he plays are in each case a witty and searching criticism of the individual whose nature invites him to adopt that particular impersonation, as Justice Clement admits admiringly at the play's conclusion; indeed in the first version Clement ends by dressing Brainworm in his robes as the truest *judge* of character on stage. Commentary on character in *Every Man In His Humour* is wholly integrated into the dramatised world of the play and closely bound up with the social relations of that world.

The Sumptuary Laws of Elizabeth's reign defined a gentleman in terms of his clothes; popular books of etiquette such as Gervase Markham's *The Gentleman's Academie* defined him in terms of his pursuits – hawking, hunting, fencing; fashionable contemporary literature defined him as cultivating a sensibility at once poetic and melancholy; Castiglione's *Book of the Courtier* defined him as attentive to the honour of others in his relations with his fellow men and scrupulously so with the opposite sex; Old Knowell in the play defines a gentleman as the product of his education and bewails at length the irresponsibility of contemporary parents who neglect to tutor their offspring in the ways of integrity, preferring to pander to their appetites.[8] Stephen is attentive to his stockings, has bought a falcon and hopes to borrow a book from his uncle Knowell that will teach him how to handle it. Above all he is obsessed with the correct tone to adopt towards his social equals and his social inferiors: he fancies developing a line in swaggering oaths for the first and pursues a policy of irascible temper with the second. Seeking to advertise his status only reveals his desperate insecurity. Matthew has a little learning and a great ambition; he has chosen a beloved quite out of his social sphere (clearly without seeking her acquiescence); his impassioned courtship after the manner of Astrophel and Stella is frustrated, which provokes his melancholy, which in turn stimulates his sonneteering. As he is dull of inspiration if intense of feeling, he has succumbed to the temptation to plagiarise the poetry of livelier minds. Kitely, though a charitable soul, as his treatment of the foundling Thomas bears witness, cannot trust his wife to lead an independent existence; her every word bespeaks her loyalty, care and devotion yet he searches through each phrase in hope of finding matter to feed his suspicions that she is adulterous. His behaviour becomes so odd that she readily believes – once Wellbred plants the idea in her mind – that her husband is guilty of sexual indiscretions on the sly. By not trusting his wife implicitly as an expression of his love for her, Kitely unwittingly brings her to the scene at Cob's house, mentioned above, which could damage her reputation, mar her innocence and put an end to her affection and sense of duty. By being ludicrously overzealous of his own honour, he dangerously maligns her. Old Knowell shows a similar want of trust in his son, despite giving him by his own standards the best of educations. He wants to keep Edward a partner of his own sheltered existence, scorns his son's love of poetry though he was himself an apt versifier in his youth, and pursues him to town expecting to find him transformed into a wanton prodigal. Edward may keep company with gulls, roarers and rascals but it is to test his sense of his own intellectual and moral difference; ironically it is his naïve father who becomes the dupe of tricksters, is suspected of immoral doings and arrested. All four – Stephen, Matthew, Kitely, Knowell – fall woefully short of contemporary ideals of a true gentleman.

Castiglione writes that the quintessential attribute of the gentleman is *sprezzatura*. This is difficult to translate, but by it he appears to mean a total confidence and ease of manner in the fact of one's prowess, accomplishments, status, sexuality, culture; it is a level of self-awareness so rigorous and of self-acceptance so complete that courtesy (in the widest possible sense of the word) becomes the whole condition of the mind, unconsciously and effortlessly governing one's every action. The effortlessness is what is most crucial and one can see immediately that all four of Jonson's would-be gentlemen are by contrast too prone to anxiety. The great strength of *Every Man In His Humour* in comparison with the other three satirical comedies is its considerate and humane approach to the follies that spring from insecurities common to the masculine mind and that can bedevil efforts at being a proper man. Knowell is a possessive fusspot of a father but his worries spring from a sense of parental responsibility that exceeds sensible proportions but which is not in itself misguided. Kitely is a man whose emotions are at war with his commonsense; as his wife observes: 'If you be sick, your own thoughts make you sick' (IV. vi. 37). Kitely is already aware of that himself: he can diagnose his condition of mind exactly and trace the growth of his disease:

> Which, as a subtle vapour, spreads itself,
> Confusedly, through every sensitive part,
> Till not a thought or motion, in the mind,
> Be free from the black poison of suspect.
>
> (II. i. 228–31)

But, as he next exclaims, 'what misery is it, to know this?' Simply *knowing* will not bring a remedy. He ends his soliloquy with a decision: 'Well, I will once more strive / In spite of this black cloud, myself to be.' He brings himself to order, yet at his next appearance is once again utterly frantic.

When Dickens produced the play he commented of his friend Forster who played Kitely: 'so far as he is concerned, there is nothing in the world but Kitely – there is no world at all; only a something in its place that begins with a "K" and ends with a "Y".[9] Much farce has been created around characters who are as totally self-obsessed as this and who in consequence do not see how absurdly at odds they are with the world in which they move. Kitely is a more complex creation however, since he sees how ridiculous he is being but cannot stop himself. Forster's annotated script has survived[10] and this shows that, while he took full advantage of the farcical possibilities of the role, he did not neglect the subtler psychological nuances. In the scene (III. iii.) where Cob races after Kitely to Justice Clement's house with the news that Wellbred has brought a 'swarm' of strangers back home, Forster notes that he would play Kitely's response ('I am sure/My sister and my wife would bid them welcome! Ha?') 'with a sort of miserable affectation of indifference (*the worst being over*)'. When Kitely discovers later that the men had not actually entered the house at the time that Cob set out, Forster promply changed the tone from miserable conviction to great excitability. Kitely dashes home and arrives (IV. i.) when Wellbred's friends are in the midst of a brawl; Forster sported a great sword in the role and drew it to end the fray. What follows when peace is restored is a discussion about the newcomer to Wellbred's circle, Edward Knowell, and Kitely is alarmed at his wife's praise of the young man's 'fair disposition' and 'excellent good parts'. Though Cash privately assures him that all the men, including Edward, have gone, Kitely is convinced otherwise: 'I'll die, but they have hid him i' the house, / Somewhere; I'll go and search.' Forster glosses this: 'Again a *hope* rises in the form of another suspicion.' The annotations suggest that Forster aimed to play the rapid fluctuations of tone here to intimate that Kitely is excited at the prospect of being within a hair's breadth of getting proof positive that he is a cuckold, that by this stage of the play he actually *wants* what he most dreads, if only to end the torture he is suffering within. That Forster continued to flourish the sword at this moment indicated that he saw Kitely as now capable of even more sinister, possibly murderous impulses. The audience would know this was all fevered imagining on Kitely's part but it would be difficult by now in the performance simply to laugh *at* the character. Henry Goodman in the 1986 RSC production achieved a different but equally complex effect with Kitely by exploiting the intimacy of the Swan Theatre: he addressed the many questions that make up Kitely's soliloquies and define his mental turmoil not inwardly to himself as rhetorical but directly to specific members of the audience. We were being privileged with his most private confidences and yet we laughed. And with every guffaw his eyes grew wider with fright and desperation: we were insulting his dignity by not taking his anguish seriously; worse, he began to suspect that we were conniving at his wife's antics behind his back. The more we laughed – and helplessly – the crueller the laughter seemed: we had become part of the world's terrible conspiracy against him, and the all-consuming nature of his obsession became not simply apparent but experienced.

Of the four young men in the play, it is a sign of Stephen and Matthew's adolescent insecurity that they quickly come under Bobadil's influence; Edward and Wellbred show greater judgement in tolerating his company for their entertainment, while never letting him see he is their fool. Bobadil's irrepressible flow of oaths and of anecdotes and schemes that vaunt his proficiency as a swordsman place him firmly in the tradition of the braggart soldier yet, like Brainworm, he is a brilliant improvisation on a classical model. The wonder of it is the beautifully sustained tone of devil-may-care insouciance, the air of complete indifference to troubles that would sap the spirit or courage of any other man. When asked if he has ever proved himself on any 'masters of defence' in London or tried their skill, his response hits a characteristic note of bemused contempt:

Alas, soon tried! You shall hear sir. Within two or three days after, they came; and by honesty, fair sir, believe me, I graced them exceedingly, showed them some two or three tricks of prevention, have purchased 'hem, since, a credit, to admiration! They cannot deny this: and yet now, they hate me, and why? Because I am excellent, and for no other vile reason on the earth. . . . Nay, for a more instance of their preposterous natures, but note, sir. They have assaulted me some three, four, five, six of them together, as I have walked alone, in divers skirts i' the town . . . where I have driven them afore me the whole length of a street, in the open view of all our gallants, pitying to hurt them, believe me . . . By myself, I could have slain them all, but I delight not in murder. (IV. v. 31–50)

The sublime nonchalance of this is an exquisite travesty of what Castiglione meant by *spezzatura*. It was cunning of Jonson to introduce another bogus soldier into the action (Brainworm in the first of his numerous disguises) to help us discriminate between conscious acting and Bobadil's identification with the role he plays which is so total that it has become a second nature. Only Downright's drubbing can eventually shake his belief that he leads a charmed life. When Dickens played Bobadil he wrote to a friend: 'I wore real armour on my throat and heart and most enormous boots and spurs – and looked like an old Spanish portrait, I assure you'; Carlyle, who saw the production, wrote tartly of 'poor little Dickens, all painted in black and red, and affecting the voice of a man of six feet'.[11] Carlyle clearly missed the point and the excellence of Dicken's conception: Bobadil is a *little* man (spiritually, if not perhaps physically) who in his own imagination is like a Spanish portrait and so powerful is the hold of mind over matter that his voice does emerge incongruously with a stentorian ring. Pete Postlethwaite in the recent RSC revival similarly stressed Bobadil's physical vulnerability to good comic effect. Cob tells us that Bobadil has had a hard night after a lengthy drunken carouse and when we first see him he is jaded and half-asleep on a bench with a handily placed bucket alongside. Postlethwaite took inspiration from this to play Bobadil as struggling throughout the play to get the world into focus through a protracted hangover; it was as if he were trying to live out a beautiful intoxicating dream of himself as Superman from which he regularly woke with a rude jolt into an all-too-painful reality.

The seedier Bobadil appears, the more amusing his verbal arabesques and fancies will become; and the greater the disparity between the Bobadil heard and the Bobadil seen, the more preposterous Stephen and Matthew will seem in taking him seriously at his own evaluation. On the brink of adulthood they are palpably unsure of their proper identities (a situation which their actual social status serves to complicate); it is not surprising that they should be seduced by Bobadil's flamboyant manner into supposing him virility personified. Imitating the great man's oaths and his tone ('Am I melancholy enough?'), taking lessons from him in fencing and smoking, listening attentively when he corrects their vocabulary and teaches them the latest in-words ('Venue! Fie. Most gross denomination, as ever I heard. Oh, the stoccata

while you live, sir' (I. iv. 142–3), simply basking in his presence
and hopefully reflecting a little of his glory gives them a sense of
belonging that they never experience elsewhere. They flatter
themselves they constitute an exclusive set until Downright rudely
calls Bobadil's bluff, beats him and leaves him bruised, humiliated
and abandoned: Matthew instantly flees in terror, while Stephen
stands by tongue-tied, offering Bobadil no assistance whatever.
Matthew has the grace to return later, nervously asking: 'I
wonder, Captain, what they will say of my going away?' Bobadil
magnanimously replies: 'Why, what should they say? But as of
a discreet gentleman? Quick, wary, respectful of nature's fair
lineaments.' He spoils the effect rather by immediately being as
magnanimous towards himself in describing the beating as 'a rude
part, a touch with soft wood, a kind of gross battery used, laid on
strongly, borne most patiently' (IV. vii. 1–8). The way he can
manipulate language to nurse his wounded self-esteem and recover
a little dignity is comic but beguilingly human. Meanwhile Stephen
having lost one hero has quickly found another: seeing Downright's
discarded cloak lying forgotten after the fray, he swathes himself
in the insignia of the conqueror and, despite Edward's warning to
take care he is not arrested for theft, goes off imitating Downright's
vigorous stride. Clearly any pattern of manhood will serve
Stephen's turn, the more aggressive its mode of expression the
better.

   The passage from youth to adulthood is a time when possible
selves are explored and discarded until a secure identity is
discovered, and the wise parent is lenient and understanding
(Jonson makes that point shrewdly in the difference of tone
between Old Knowell and the genial Justice Clement, whose
relaxed humour keeps the follies and misdemeanours of the other
characters in a proper perspective and teaches the audience a
sensible and sensitive response). Brainworm's skill as an actor is
in assuming a range of roles and appropriate voices with the switch
of a costume ('Oh, that thou should'st disguise thy language so,
as I should not know thee' V. i. 147–8) which he does as occasion
demands and largely for the sheer pleasure of exercising his wit
and imagination; this serves to offset the more anxious exploration
of their identities by most of the other characters. What surprises
in this context is Jonson's decision to excise from the Folio version
of the play the vigorous defence of poetry as the finest possible

expression of a gentleman's worth and spirit which he gave to Edward Knowell's prototype, Lorenzo Junior, in the Quarto. There when Matheo stands condemned by Clement as a scribbler, Lorenzo senior turns to his son with the snide observation 'you see / How abjectly your poetry is rank'd in general opinion' (V. i. p. 56) and Lorenzo junior, with an assurance clearly born of deep inner conviction, shows his father that it is a sign of the decadence of their age that it should make no distinction between Matthew or any other poetaster and 'a true poet: than which reverend name / Nothing can more adorn humanity' (V. i. p. 57). In the Folio version it is Clement who answers Old Knowell's tetchy aside ('Nay, no speech or act of mine be drawn against such as profess it worthily. They are not born every year, as an alderman' V. i. 235–7) and Edward says gratefully 'Sir, you have saved me the labour of a defence' (l. 244). John Caird in directing the recent RSC production did right in restoring the earlier version of this moment to his acting text.[12] It is the one episode in the play when father and son speak to each other and the old man stands justifiably rebuked by the young one: Edward has come of age, has an independent mind and will speak respectfully but firmly in defence of his personal values. The speech is essential to the completion of the psychological patterning of the play.

If *Every Man In His Humour* has remained popular in our theatre and attracted fine actors to its performance, it is because it opens up beyond contemporary Elizabethan satire into a dramatisation of psychological dilemmas common to any age; and in approaching that larger theme Jonson brings to his comic invention a humanity that often seems cruelly withheld from his later Elizabethan plays, *Every Man Out of His Humour*, *Cynthia's Revels* and *The Poetaster*. He had here created a comedy of character that owed nothing to the Elizabethan fashion for romantic intrigue and little overtly to the tradition of classical comedy. The character in these four plays that seems most to anticipate the way that Jonson would forge through to his great Jacobean cycle of comedies is Brainworm, the one character in *Every Man In His Humour* that some critics have found least developed. If Martin Seymour-Smith is right in his conjecture that Burbage played the role initially, then clearly it became a vehicle for a virtuoso display of acting skills.[13] Acting is an obsession with Brainworm: it is the essence of the man. He relishes deception and thrives on the risks it necessitates taking. Yet his deceptions have an undeniably salutary effect in the play, engineering complications the better to achieve a satisfactory resolution. In this he is a useful device for controlling and developing the action, providing clever transitions from one episode to another. But in performance the role quite transcends its obvious function. And in doing so it becomes oddly disturbing for the audience: knavery is a source of delight, because Brainworm carries it off with shameless exuberance; moreover his tricks are often bound up with judgement of the other characters – judgements which Clement, the voice of authority, ultimately endorses. There is nothing schematic about the moral patterning here: Jonson is exploiting our irrepressible joy in a virtuoso performer in order to challenge our powers of discrimination. As it happens Brainworm's skill is directed at achieving sensible, decent objectives. What if his intentions had been more sinister and his sport been not with follies but with crime?

3
A First Interlude:
'Sejanus his Fall'

It is tempting to argue that Jonson found a mature style for comedy as a consequence of attempting unsuccessfully to write a tragedy. This would be unfair to *Sejanus*, which is a finer play than this comment would suggest; also the elements of what went to make *Volpone* the remarkable innovation that it is were all present in embryonic form in Jonson's Elizabethan comedies, but there they were isolated, chance conceptions and had not yet found a right relation to each other. Shakespeare invariably turns at climactic moments in his plays, as Anne Barton has superbly demonstrated, to 'the idea of the play' itself, to the root facts of performance.[1] His characters, seeking to define a sudden acute awareness of the self, generally express that perception in metaphors about acting, about players that strut and fret upon the stage of life. As with all good metaphysical conceits, the effect is to sharpen one's sense of the differences between the ideas brought into a sudden relation only to give greater immediacy to one's sense of the manifest similarities. For the audience the impact is at once to make them both conscious of themselves as present at a theatre and conscious of the artifice of performance while bringing them into a greater imaginative empathy with the characters in their moments of crisis. The purposeful theatricality actually enhances the psychological verisimilitude. In Shakespeare the technique works largely through verbal metaphor (though the utterance may accompany or eluci-date a remarkable gesture or activity as when the conspirators bathe their hands in Caesar's blood while Cassius exclaims 'How

31

many ages hence/Shall this our lofty scene be acted over / In states unborn and accents yet unknown!').[2] The exceptions to this pattern occur when Shakespeare uses the device of the play-within-the-play as in *Hamlet* or *The Tempest*, when the whole process of theatre with astonishing precision of reference becomes a symbol both of the world of the play and of the protagonist's mind. Jonson's access to a mature dramatic style seems to have been accompanied by a growing awareness of the value to the playwright of a technique of purposeful theatricality, but where Shakespeare worked chiefly on the level of imagery, Jonson worked principally on the level of action and that in ways which threw into increasingly sharp relief the relationship of actor to audience. Shakespeare explores images of playing to bring a close identification between the actor and his role; Jonson, always the moralist, appears to have been fascinated and troubled by acting as conscious deception, by the process of theatre that elevates wilful impersonation to the status of an art. His genius lay in finding a dramatic method that would instil that private dilemma into his audiences. His plays in consequence became strategies that at once attract and alarm. It is often argued that Jonson's plays act better than they read: certainly the sublety of their effect is dependent on the fact of *performance* and on the audience's awareness of itself as *participating* in the art we call theatre.

The most memorable moments in Jonson's Elizabethan comedies are those that involve a deliberate exposure of the artifice of performance. Three are of particular importance to an appreciation of *Sejanus*: the travesty of the conventions of romantic comedy in *The Case is Altered* which seems designed to make an audience question why it should indulge in such escapist nonsense; the presence of an on-stage audience in the last act of *Cynthia's Revels* and throughout *Every Man Out of His Humour* to enliven the theatre-audience's sense of drama as a participatory experience requiring of them judgement and discrimination; and, crucially, Brainworm's zest for creative role-playing which emphasises the extent to which firstly Stephen and Matthew are overparted (since they are incapable of sustaining their chosen roles with the necessary degree of confidence) and secondly Bobadil is overly identified with an assumed persona which is incongruous with his background, appearance and essential temperament. Interestingly it is Matthew, Stephen and Bobadil's efforts totally to commit

themselves to their respective roles that are their undoing; Brainworm by contrast *presents* a role, conscious that it is artifice and
no likeness of himself. This gives him a necessary detachment
from which to calculate to a nicety how much detail to develop to
convince different audiences of the truth of his portrayals. His
primary concern is acceptance by his audience; theirs self-projec-
tion and display.

   This was an apt complex of ideas to pursue further when Jonson
decided to dramatise Tacitus' account of the life and fall of
Sejanus since he chose as thematic centre for his play to explore
Machiavelli's theories of politics, and Machiavelli in *The Prince*
had advocated that the ideal ruler should cultivate the art of acting
and learn to be a master at feigning. Jonson was not, of course,
the first dramatist to see the potential for good theatre in that
recommendation: the 1590s had produced an array of Make-evils,
great actors all, in Barabas, Mortimer and the Guise, Aaron and
Richard III (to list but Marlowe's and Shakespeare's creations).
By cunning, malpractice and calculated acts of violence the
Machiavel fostered anarchy so that he might seize what opportunities for power surfaced in consequence of the unrest; he sustained
with consummate skill a public persona quite at variance with his
private self and relished his proficiency in doing so. The type,
drawing on the tradition of the comic devils of medieval drama,
made for danger in the theatre: he was exciting for the sheer
energy of his mind and alarming for the depths of depravity that
mind could reach after in its obsession with power. The character's
end was tragic because he became bumptiously confident of his
expertise or bored with his capacity for success then met his match
unexpectedly or got caught out by his own ingenious plotting. All
five Machiavels mentioned are noticeably 'outsiders' who aspire
to absolute rule; but all, in achieving it, are found to lack the
vision that is necessary if authority is to be more than a display of
power. The fashion for that style of drama quickly passed,
presumably because the structural pattern of relentless rise and
spectacular fall became predictable and the rhetoric of ambition
hackneyed by imitation. Shakespeare in Bolingbroke, Henry V
and the Duke in *Measure for Measure* later began to examine the
anguish of rulers required to use Machiavellian tactics as an
expression of their authority and to maintain general order in the
state. John Marston sought (firstly with Piero in *Antonio's Revenge*)

to satirise the type of stage Machiavel as predictable in a different way, as possessing energy but not *flexibility* of mind, so that once he was committed to that role his bloody demise was ineluctable and the last laugh was on him for being so short-sighted. The interest for Jonson would appear to be in the fact that by 1603 the Machiavellian villain had hardened into a stage-type which an audience could comfortably 'place': reduced to a convention he was no longer dangerous.

The opening act of *Sejanus*[3] must have been disconcerting for its initial audience to say the least. The protagonist establishes no immediate rapport with the audience in the manner of Barabas or Richard III; instead he is seen briefly passing along in a procession surrounded by his spies, henchmen and sycophants seeking to buy positions at court. The stage meanwhile is dominated by a group of senators who comment adversely on his rapid rise to power as the emperor's favourite and see him as exemplary of the way current standards in politics have declined under Tiberius' rule. In the next scene we watch him manipulating a subordinate to do his will: what Sejanus terms 'making' a man. There is none of the virtuoso display of wit with which Richard courts Lady Anne or Barabas allays Abigail's scruples about entering the convent in order to recover the Jew's hidden treasure; instead Eudemus is all-too-eager to comply, being honoured by Sejanus' attentions. These, since Eudemus is physician to the women of the imperial family, consist largely of lewd enquiries about the more intimate details of his patients' well-being. After a brief soliloquy in which Sejanus outlines how he will use Eudemus to seduce Livia (his rival Drusus' wife) on his behalf and thus get her aid in poisoning her husband, the stage fills for an audience with the emperor in which Sejanus' role is confined entirely to flattery of Tiberius' god-like perspicacity. As the court disperses, there is a battle for precedence between Sejanus and Drusus, the emperor's son; Drusus strikes Sejanus and, when he refuses to draw his sword and fight, taunts him for his 'cold spirits' as a 'dull camel' who merits a lingering death by crucifixion, the punishment reserved for slaves and traitors. Left alone, Sejanus speaks a terse six-line soliloquy, tense with hatred and lethal intent (I. i. 564–581). Where is the customary dynamism of the stage-Machiavel, the humour that betokens an absolute self-confidence, or the sheer physical command of stage-space enabling him to direct, at times even manipulate, the movement of the other characters within it? Sejanus by comparison is decidedly lacklustre; he is upstaged by everyone except menials; there is none of the expansive rhetoric that might give us a sense of the man's imaginative capacity since, of his two soliloquies, one is coldly factual, the other fraught with malice. The flamboyance of conventional villains is absent yet there is no denying his power since Sejanus is continually the focus in the dialogue for everyone's outrage, anger, disgust (always excepting Tiberius who basks in his adulation): 'He is the now court-god; . . . 'Tis he/Makes us our day, or night' (I. i. 203–7). The one scene which shows Sejanus in pursuit of his objectives, his suborning of Eudemus, demonstrates that power in operation to be a matter of backstairs work, of behind-the-arras gossip and cajoling, a tricking of others with vague promises of power ('Thou art a man, made, to make Consuls' I. i. 351). It is the sordid reality of power politics as advocated by Machiavelli that is Jonson's subject, not, as the theatrical convention would have it, the seductive glamour.

Machiavelli in *Il Principe* recommends secrecy and covert dealings, subtle acting and deception, the use of others to perform the most heinous acts one deems necessary so as to save one's own reputation, the cultivating of certain animal-like traits in one's nature (preferably those of the fox and the lion), and the stimulating of every beast-like tendency in others to make them prompt to respond to one's persuasions. One is tempted in reading Machiavelli's treatise to question what is the *value* of the power these attributes will accomplish and this seems increasingly the drift of Jonson's debate within the play. Sejanus has reached the height of power possible to him as a gentleman of Rome; his only hope of further advancement is through marriage with Livia, which would make him a member of the imperial family and thus give his ambitions a point of vantage in aiming to be emperor. Tiberius has encouraged Sejanus' rise thus far but checks at his marriage proposals; he advises Sejanus to pursue modesty and caution, talking as if some great mystique attaches to the imperial name in the minds of the senate and the citizens of Rome which it would be sacrilege not to honour. The idea of this respected *élite* does not accord well with what we have actually seen of Livia herself (she seems to value an artfully coloured complexion more than her husband's honour, status or life), of Germanicus's sons who are heirs to the throne or of Tiberius; there is nothing about their characters, as Jonson presents them, that merits this prestige. Actually Tiberius recognises this fact: he enjoys asserting he is no more than merely human ('style not us / Or lord, or mighty, who profess ourself/The servant of the senate' I. i. 391–3) and despises those senators who delude themselves into thinking otherwise. Sejanus' dilemma is that for the sake of his ambitions he has to respect the mystique of imperial office while recognising the gross and all-too-fallible nature of the present emperor. He is the dupe of his own lust for power since what he is pursuing is palpably an illusion.

Jonson dramatises this blindspot in Sejanus' thinking by a subtle ploy: he does not give Sejanus any of the customary rhetoric and hyperboles defining ambition until the realities of the political situation in Rome have been firmly sketched in, and then not in a soliloquy but when Sejanus is embracing Livia and scheming with her to assassinate her husband. He shares his aspirations with her as his technique of seduction:

> Such a spirit as yours,
> Was not created for the idle second
> To a poor flash, as Drusus; but to shine
> Bright, as the moon, among the lesser lights,
> And share the sovereignty of all the world.
> Then Livia triumphs in her proper sphere,
> When she, and her Sejanus shall divide
> The name of Caesar; and Augusta's star
> Be dimmed with glory of a brighter beam:
> When Agrippina's fires are quite extinct,
> And the scarce-seen Tiberius borrows all
> His little light from us, whose folded arms
> Shall make one perfect orb.   (II. i. 33–45)

The irony is that, as the wife of Tiberius's heir, Livia is already possessed of the very position Sejanus is offering her; he has merely decked out her present reality with the mystique of power and she is too infatuated with his manner to judge his matter properly. One is not sure at this point whether Sejanus believes in the force of his own rhetoric or whether he is being cynical, adopting a tactic he knows will succeed with a silly, gullible victim.

As Sejanus' hopes come closer in his estimation to being realised, so his soliloquies become more frequent and lengthy, their rhetoric more extravagant.

> Swell, swell, my joys: and faint not to declare
> Yourselves, as ample, as your causes are.
> I did not live, till now; this my first hour:
> Wherein I see my thoughts reached by my power.
> But this, and grip my wishes. Great, and high,
> The world knows only two, that's Rome, and I.
> My roof receives me not; 'tis air I tread:
> And, at each step, I feel my advanced head
> Knock out a star in heav'n! Reared to this height,
> All my desires seem modest, poor and slight,
> That did before sound impudent: 'tis place,
> Not blood, discerns the noble and the base.
> Is there not something more, than to be Caesar?
>   (V. i. 1–13)

Beside the practice of imperial statecraft as demonstrated in the play by Tiberius, this is plainly ridiculous: rule has been shown to fall very short of the transcendent values these images evoke. Sejanus is deluding himself, as he had deluded Livia previously, with myths about power: this is proof positive of his incapacity for actual rule. What we have here is the familiar idiom of the stage Machiavel but carried to an excess, where it becomes a comic critique of the original style. The effect is to make Sejanus appear to be acting a role for which he lacks the necessary qualities: stage presence, self-awareness, brio. He is like Bobadil, a travesty of the type he seeks to emulate, because he has completely identified with it as his chosen role, become in fact type-cast and lost all flexibility of technique.

The yardstick by which to assess Sejanus' failure is Tiberius. It is an irony that adds to the absurdity of Sejanus' position that he never contemplates the possibility that, just as he uses others for his ends and despises them for their tractability, so Tiberius may be using and despising him. Sejanus believes he alone can read Tiberius' mind and can influence his attitudes and moods – a view he persists in even after Tiberius has signally failed to be influenced

by Sejanus' persuasions to let him marry Livia; most other characters in the play find the emperor a mystery and his precise motives
and intentions difficult to gauge. This ruler remains a lion by virtue
of deploying all the qualities of the fox: trickery and feigning are
his essential nature. Tiberius is so supremely confident of his
technique that he once actually reveals to Sejanus the extent of
his capacity to act roles, knowing that Sejanus will be too
enamoured of his own perception of the emperor to take due note
of the real significance of the scene he devises for his favourite's
education. They discuss Agrippina's household, the sedition that
she seems to be fostering and debate ways the threats she poses
might be contained (II. ii). Tiberius plays for the moment the man
Sejanus believes him to be: ageing, querulous, fearful for his own
safety, anxiously dependent on Sejanus' advice to soothe his fretful
state. Asked by Sejanus what he feels inclined to do, Tiberius
promptly suggests extreme measures; Sejanus questions the advis-
ability of so proceeding and recommends craftier moves:

> Thus, with slight
> You shall disarm them first, and they (in night
> Of their ambition) not perceive the train,
> Till, in the engine, they are caught, and slain.
>
> (II. ii. 266–9)

Tiberius hesitates, asking 'Is there no way to bind them by deserts?'
but Sejanus is implacable: 'Sir, wolves do change their hair, but
not their hearts" (ll. 271–2). Sitting in judgement on Agrippina's
circle, Sejanus has condemned himself, did he but realise it, and
shows Tiberius how best to proceed against him. Tiberius on the
instant changes his tone completely; becoming briskly efficient, he
admits his whole manner until now has been nothing but acting
and that he was seeking confirmation of policies he has already
decided on

> We can no longer
> Keep on our mask to thee, our dear Sejanus;
> Thy thoughts are ours, in all, and we but proved
> Their voice, in our designs . . . (II. ii. 278–81)

Sejanus' confidence that he has the measure of Tiberius' mind is absurdly misplaced. Instead Tiberius shows himself to be more dangerous, the more he demonstrates how consummate an actor he is and after this moment in the play one marvels at the versatility of his shape-changing: solicitous in advising Sejanus how best to care for his reputation even while plotting a character assassination of his one-time favourite that will lead rapidly to his actual execution; flattering Macro's intelligence ('Macro is sharp and apprehends') by giving him swift instructions on how to 'spy/Inform, and chastise' in order to work Sejanus' downfall, while recognising full well that that intelligence is too prodigious ever to merit trust (III. ii.). The same observation might be made of Tiberius: it is a masterstroke in the play's construction that Jonson could confidently assume that the character had made sufficient impact with the audience that he could remove the emperor from the action after Act Three yet still allow Tiberius credibly to stage-manage every other character's movements throughout the remaining scenes. Each intricate development in the plotting that leads to Sejanus' demise has been calculated by Tiberius to keep everyone involved guessing about a possible resolution. The whole conception shows how utterly he despises the creatures who inhabit Rome: they are as flies to his wanton godhead which he toys with then kills for sport. As the mark both of his power and his indifference, he retreats to Capri; there is no need for his physical presence in Rome: the stage-action becomes wholly symbolic through Acts Four and Five of the workings of the emperor's imagination, at once brilliant, perverse, savage and witty. This is statecraft as Machiavelli envisaged it. Note how, whenever Tiberius' acting is at its most super-subtle, Jonson invariably signals the fact by having the dialogue refer to him as 'Prince' or 'Prince-like' and usually in close proximity to a phrase like 'rarely dissembled', as on his first entry (I. i. 395). Beside Tiberius' evil genius the efforts of the conventional stage-Machiavel appear like so much comic posturing, as in Sejanus himself.

It might be objected that this interpretation of *Sejanus* is pushing theatrical analogies too far. But there is one further device within the play, yet to be commented on, that precisely encourages such an approach. This is the on-stage audience of senators surrounding Silius and Arruntius through whom periodically most of the action in the public scenes is mediated. Cordatus and Mitis in *Every Man*

Out Of His Humour were altogether too knowing and so robbed that comedy of much of its tension and element of surprise. The Roman senators are quickly established as decent sorts, variously distinguished as shrewd, frank, brusque, intelligent in that they can accurately read Sejanus' actions, infer his motives and guess his larger schemes, even if they are powerless to forestall or prevent them. Tiberius' moves continually perplex them ('I am not Oedipus enough / To understand this sphinx' III. i. 64–5); he ever eludes 'placing' in the way they can categorise and indeed do characterise Sejanus, Drusus, or the late Germanicus: 'Tiberius' heart / Lies a thought farther, than another man's' (III. i. 97–8). All they can do is admire his skill – 'Well acted, Caesar'; 'Well dissembled' – while being profoundly disturbed by what that skill intimates: 'If this man / Had but a mind allied unto his words / How blest a fate were it to us, and Rome?' (I. i. 400–2). Their uncertainty challenges our powers of discrimination even as it alerts us to the originality of Jonson's handling of the emperor: he is not cast in any conventional mould for portraying evil. If this were the extent of the function of the on-stage audience in the drama, then the device might appear heavy-handed, but the play abounds in actor-audience situations of a complexity that begins to compel the theatre-audience imaginatively to engage with the horror of living in a police state under the control of a merciless tyrant. Sejanus' henchmen, whose actions in public in the opening scene form the main substance of the play-within-the-play that is closely watched by Silius, Arruntius and their friends, are themselves adept as spies and informers at turning what other characters believe to be confidential, private encounters into performances for hidden audiences who make their presence suddenly known to the performers' cost. No one can be sure when he is truly alone and when the object of another's scrutiny: 'May I think / And not be racked? What danger is't to dream?' Arruntius cries out in anguish; 'Nothing has privilege 'gainst the violent ear / No place, no day, no hour (we see) is free' (IV. iv. 304–5 and 311–12). Silius and Cordus are both summoned before the senate and required to prove their innocence and integrity for an audience inclined to judge their every word and action differently from the interpretation they themselves assert. Afer, the public orator, at Sejanus' bidding, can eloquently justify the most malicious and vindictive criticism as soundly reasoned, which leaves their victims only the dignity of silence or suicide. What the constantly changing patterns of actor-audience relationships in the play actualise for us power-fully is the nightmare of living in a world where reason and judgement are not a matter of cool, objective appraisal but are swayed by subjective political affiliations. What is *real* in this world where every person's action is either known to be or can suddenly be deemed to be clever *acting*? The challenge to the theatre-audience's powers of perception is acute: how can we detect the tone of sincerity? We may feel secure in the presence of Arruntius' blustering good nature but throughout he is condemned to the passive role of observer; for all his intelligence and commonsense, he is quite impotent to affect the course of events. Jonson creates considerable tension in his audience by showing the voice of common decency repeatedly gagged: no gesture of protest is possible in Tiberius' Rome, so complete is the emperor's control of the lives and minds of his subjects. This is the reality behind Machiavelli's theories of statecraft.

Critics have often taken exception to the presence of so much potential comedy in *Sejanus*, considering it destructive of tragic decorum. Livia's obsession with fucus and dentifrice, ceruse and pomatum and Sejanus' inflated ego in the jubilation that precedes his downfall are the usual evidence mustered here. One could argue that most of the last act in performance would provoke laughter – but of a tense, not to say hysterical tone. Jonson was invariably critical of dramatists who deployed moments of sensational spectacle, yet, closely following his source materials, he chose to include the scene of the ritual to placate the goddess Fortune with its mechanical marvel of the statue that 'averts' its head, an episode which is an odd mixture of solemnity and bathos, as is the whole treatment at that same point in the play of the prodigies in nature foretelling Sejanus' doom, where satire of similar passages in Shakespeare's *Julius Caesar* hovers at the edges of the conception.[4] Given the godless society Jonson has created and Sejanus' own frank atheism, the sudden intrusion of piety and superstition inevitably strikes one as cynical and absurd, as Sejanus himself is the first to admit. Then there is the scene where Macro is in haste to get his plans for Sejanus' overthrow properly established: he needs the help of the consul, Regulus, but Regulus officiously takes himself off on his various errands and is never present on stage when Macro thinks of the next project in which

Ben Jonson

urgently to employ him. The senators meanwhile are all a-dither
not knowing how to read the political signs as distinct from all the
prodigies; confusion reigns as to who is in Tiberius' favour, who
fallen from grace; and Laco, the born toady, speaks for all when
he deplores these 'forked tricks': 'Would he would tell us whom
he loves, or hates, / That we might follow, without fear, or doubt'
(IV. iv. 424–5). Later when the other consul, Trio, lets slip in
private to a friend that Sejanus is about to receive 'the tribunitial
dignity', the stage is a-buzz with gossip: 'What's the news?' – 'I'll
tell you / But you must swear to keep it secret' (V. v. 417–18).
Sejanus is visited by his arch-enemy Macro, but is deceived by his
unctuous performance into supposing him 'honest and worthy'.
The senators cannot now race to their meeting fast enough ('See,
Sanquinius! / With his slow belly, and his dropsy! look, / What
toiling haste he makes!' V. vi. 454–6). As the majestic sentences
of Tiberius' letter fluctuate between praise of Sejanus and blame,
so the senators crowd round the favourite or slide away along the
seats to keep their distance, the ebb and flow of their movement
capturing exactly their abject servility. Denounced, Sejanus is
rushed from the stage to his death, speechless. Even the climax of
it all, because described not seen, is oddly grotesque: Sejanus'
death and dismemberment at the hands of the mob; Macro's
demonic zeal that does not hesitate even at the murder of his
rival's children; the grief of Sejanus' estranged wife, Apicata, that
unleashes a gross sentimentality in the mob who now 'wish him
collected and created new' (V. vi. 890). The tone, meticulously
controlled, is poised between the horrific and the absurd, and the
effect is to rob all the characters at the close of any vestige of
human dignity. This is too sustained an effect for it not to be
calculated. It is horrific because we realise increasingly that
everyone is being ruthlessly manipulated by Tiberius' evil will: he
knows everyone involved through and through and can effortlessly
devise this grandly intricate scenario while despising the lot of
them for their predictability, their 'flat servility'. How ironic it
seems now that, when we first saw Tiberius, he was rejecting any
approaches that suggested he possessed god-like attributes! In
many classical tragedies, the patterning of events that make up
the plot is designed to show the power and immanence of a god:
Apollo in Sophocles' *King Oedipus* is everywhere felt if nowhere
actually seen. Tiberius achieves this omniscience, this immanence,

as *Sejanus* develops; he expresses himself in the history he
masterminds in Rome through cruelty and cynicism. The emperor's
cunning is at various points in the play described as his 'art';
Jonson's artistry in the last two acts holds up a mirror to Tiberius'
essential nature as a true Machiavel, even as the stage-Machiavel,
Sejanus, is reduced to a clownish puppet and then to abject silence
by this display of totalitarian politics at their most insidious. It is
the mark of Tiberius' genius that it has made all values relative in
the interests of absolute rule and by the end of the play we are
trapped in a dilemma about how properly to respond: to laugh
would imply complicity with Tiberius, yet it is difficult to feel tragic
sympathy for individuals who are such willing stooges, victims of
their own will to power. Ultimately we are trapped by Jonson's
artful strategies, his complexities of tone, and left like Arruntius
and his peers caught between outrage and impotence. *Sejanus* is a
savage and brilliant conception: it merits revival.

4
'Volpone'

When at the zenith of his fortunes in the play Volpone at last has Celia all to himself and he searches for words to express his height of ecstasy, the image that comes most readily to mind is a memory of himself as a child-actor and the idol of all the female members of his audience:

> I am, now, as fresh,
> As hot, as high, and in as jovial plight
> As when, in that so celebrated scene,
> As recitation of our comedy,
> For entertainment of the great Valois
> I acted young Antinous; and attracted
> The eyes and ears of all the ladies present,
> T' admire such graceful gesture, note and footing.
>
> (III. vii. 157–64)[1]

It is an expansively lyrical moment and remarkable for its concern with the recollection of times past when the language of most of the characters in the play is preoccupied obsessively with the immediate present, the *thisness* of things and of people, which they each hope in the fullness of time to turn to their personal advantage. Seeking through past experience for a like sense of being wholly at one with himself, Volpone recalls being a centre of adulation for his skills in impersonation. This child is distinctly

father to the man: acting, as we have seen throughout the previous
acts, is the essence of Volpone's nature; he is a virtuoso. So much
so that, as his seduction of Celia continues, we sense (given our
knowledge of his brilliance at impersonation) a profound irony
behind his promises to her of unimaginable bliss. True sexual
fulfilment brings with it an enhanced awareness of the self; it is less
transcendence that Volpone seeks than effortless transformation, a
complete loss of self in an unending succession of roles; life will
be continual *play*:

>   my dwarf shall dance,
> My eunuch sing, my fool make up the antic.
> Whil'st we, in changèd shapes, act Ovid's tales,
> Thou, like Europa now, and I like Jove,
> Then I like Mars and thou like Erycine;
> So of the rest, till we have quite run through,
> And wearied all the fables of the gods.
> Then will I have thee in more modern forms . . .
> And I will meet thee in as many shapes.   (III. vii. 219–33)

In all the 'sums of pleasure' Volpone offers Celia, he never includes
a constant heart and mind: the self he proffers is elusive and
illusory. The idea of all these acting opportunities so possesses
Volpone's imagination that he quite fails to see how bizarrely
inappropriate the whole catalogue of roles is for Celia: he tempts
her with images of pagan carnality and more modern stereotypes
suggestive of sexual abandon ('quick Negro or cold Russian'), all
intimating that he sees her as 'one of our most *artful* courtesans',
when Celia is a dutiful, god-fearing, eminently bourgeois *wife*.
What adds to the comedy is our growing awareness that deception
is so fundamental a part of Volpone's thinking that he cannot but
suppose Celia's chastely virtuous manner is *assumed*: married to
an ass the like of Corvino, she could not be genuinely submissive;
behind that icy front must lurk a rampant imagination. Simple-
minded Celia may appear beside the super-subtle Volpone, but
her response to his bewildering display of acted selves goes right
to the heart of the moral issue he confronts her with: she questions
whether he has 'ears that will be pierced, or eyes / That can be
opened, a heart may be touched' and, most significant of all, 'any
part that yet sounds man about you' (III. vii. 240–2). To Celia,

Volpone, the self-absorbed actor, is altogether too fantastic to be human.

Ironically it is not Celia but Volpone who is seduced by his own wild imaginings. What is more, there is nothing truly original about them. The scenarios for the promised orgy are borrowed from Ovid, even Volpone's song is plagiarised from Catullus. The actor's creativity is of necessity presentational: it is always dependent for its material on the art and vision of others; his skills in consequence are continually circumscribed by that need. Volpone is invariably and often dangerously at a loss, as in the scene with Celia, when he is separated from his master-dramatist, Mosca, the parasite.

Parasites in Roman comedy survive by flattering other characters' views of themselves and of the world in return for a good meal; they are essentially harmless toadies. Mosca serves this function for Volpone, continually heaping praise on his master for his histrionic displays: as John Creaser observes, 'even [Volpone's] most secret roles enjoy the appreciation of Mosca, who in his connoisseurship is alone an audience worth impressing'.[2] But Mosca also has affinities with the crafty slaves of Plautus' and Terence's plays, men who use their shrewd knowledge of their masters to shape an intrigue which brings about a resolution that contents most of the characters involved and gains the slaves either better conditions or freedom. The situations that form the plot in the later stages of these comedies are largely of their devising. The wily slave takes on the role of dramatist, creating a scenario in which his trusting younger master, the son of the house, consciously becomes an actor; his older master, the paterfamilias, is innocently caught up in the action, the logic of which often compels him into situations and decisions that run counter to his own preferred aims. Volpone may be a first-class actor but he is utterly dependent on Mosca to create the scenarios in which he can demonstrate his art. Noticeably Jonson keeps silent about whether it was master or man who first had the inspiration to set up the play they have been performing and perfecting for the past three years. Act One of Jonson's comedy establishes the basic scheme within which daily they improvise variations: Volpone shams dying and Mosca encourages a host of legacy-hunters to bring lucrative presents in the hope of being declared heir to the near-deceased. Volpone acquires ever more wealth, while as the months pass the suitors strive to outdo the lavishness of each others' gifts ('Here I have brought a bag of bright chequins / Will quite weigh down his plate' I. iv. 69–70) and Mosca gets yet more audacious in the scenarios he devises in which the suitors all unwittingly play a prescribed role. Any skill expertly demonstrated excites admiration and there is no denying that the panache with which master and man carry off their deceptions is thrilling to watch; but if Act One is well played, then we should, along with our delight in Volpone and Mosca's vitality, begin to sense tensions in their relationship too.

Once Volpone dons his costume and make-up and assumes his role, we find it imposes severe restraints on his boisterous self. It is a commonplace of theatrical gossip that actors enjoy a good death scene and will milk it for every sensational effect; yet senile mouthings and protracted death throes are all that is allowed Volpone in two of the three scenarios. Focus of attention though it is, Volpone's is predominantly a *mimed* role; he is the dumb-show for which Mosca acts as presenter, creating a context of meaning which Volpone's motions must then exemplify. Though ostensibly Mosca gives himself the subsidiary role of obsequious servant, like the servant-figures of *commedia dell'arte* he has a happy knack of developing that role as a vehicle for his many technical accomplishments; by the third visit, Corvino's, he indulges in a dazzling *lazzo* enacting a whole deathbed scene about a supposed signing of Volpone's will in which in his one person he caricatures Corbaccio, Voltore and his master. Where the scenarios steadily constrict Volpone's power of invention, they liberate Mosca's. He is the complete artist-performer: he controls, shapes, paces, dictates the tone of each of the scenes with the suitors and, by the time he encourages Corvino to join him in shouting abuse in the ears of a supposedly deaf Volpone ('You may be louder yet; a culverin / Discharged in his ear would hardly bore it' I. v. 63–4), he has turned their joint enterprise into a practical joke at his master's expense. Volpone chooses to interpret the episode as witty exuberance: 'My divine Mosca! / Thou hast today outgone thyself' (I. v. 84–5). A shrewd spectator might well read another meaning into 'outgone thyself', especially one versed in the tradition of Roman comedy and *commedia*, where slaves and servants repeatedly, and sometimes cruelly, upstage their social superiors, reducing them to objects of mockery. Mosca has framed each of the scenarios with Voltore, Corbaccio and Corvino to expose not only their stupidity but also their inherent cruelty: Voltore's callous indifference when, in the face of a series of convincing death-rattles from Volpone, all he is anxious for is assurance that he is 'inscribed his heir, for certain'; Corbaccio's murderous intent in bringing a specially prepared opiate that is clearly poisoned; and Corvino's willingness that Mosca should stifle Volpone at his 'discretion' providing he personally is not present to be implicated in the deed. Having been taught by Jonson through these episodes to discriminate degrees of cruelty, one cannot but suspect the relish Mosca takes in discomforting his patron in the final encounter: horseplay is rarely free of malice.

It is not surprising, given the claustrophobia, restraints, pressures, lurking tensions imposed on him by his 'performances' indoors, that Volpone should for respite seek the freedom of the Venetian piazzas. What is astonishing in view of his wholly successful impersonation at home is that he does not trust that he will be unrecognised if he goes abroad in his own very vigorous person. Hearing of Corvino's exquisite wife, Celia ('Bright as your gold! and lovely as your gold!' I. v. 114), he decides on the instant that he must see her; Mosca promptly recommends a disguise and Volpone as readily agrees on the condition that his new role will allow him to 'maintain mine own shape still the same (I. v. 129). This impersonation is to avoid caricature and be as like him as possible while being manifestly a role. He reappears as a mountebank, Scoto of Mantua, an odd declension for a magnifico. Jonson now halts his plot awhile for what is one of the longest scenes in the play, seemingly to explore Volpone's transformation. Mountebank is a fitting alter ego: acting is his means of survival as is Volpone's; he too plays with people's hopes – his simples, potions, restoratives promising renewal of vigour and beauty. At heart his clients know that he is peddling illusions, that he is a charlatan, yet their longing to escape the processes of age lets them be seduced by his cunning words. They know he is a knave and he knows that they know and that what they know is the truth; and so his performance grows out of a kind of pact between mountebank and audience that he will work to suspend their judgement, his wit and linguistic brio charming forth their acquiescence despite their initial scepticism; for the duration of his act they *will* him to transform their perceptions and make them believe the impossible. It is a most sophisticated actor-audience relationship that Jonson illustrates here, but it is one where all the actor's intellectual effort (and Volpone's sales patter is spectacular in its flow of verbal inventions) is directed at ends which are wholly escapist: making his audience believe they are anything but the fools they patently are in standing there wasting the very time that is the prime source of their anxieties. The mountebank, like Volpone himself, must utterly despise his audience while relishing his absolute control over them. The episode intimates far darker psychological resonances behind the play-acting of Act One than are sensed there, yet this is brilliantly done through a scene that sustains a tone of light, airy fancy. Volpone gives a superb performance as Scoto but, even while admiring the artistry and verve, one cannot suppress the notion that it is all a rather lavish effort simply to get a glimpse of Celia. As the action of the play develops it becomes increasingly apparent that Volpone can express himself only through a waste of his talents, faculties, possessions. When later he gives Celia jewels as a prologue to his attempted seduction, he is at a loss to define for her their actual value because they have no obvious use except to squander as a display of one's indifference to wealth: 'A gem but worth a private patrimony / Is nothing: we will eat such at a meal' (III. vii. 200–1). Meaning is given to Volpone's life only by flamboyant gestures, the cost of which he disdains. The precise cost of his act as mountebank is a good drubbing from Corvino. Scoto's great flight of fantasy is suddenly cut short by the arrival of the jealous husband who sees the whole set-up (accurately) as a lecher's device for making an approach to his Celia. Corvino reduces the grand romantic escapade to the level of the bedroom farce of *commedia* and is furious at finding himself cast in the ludicrous role of Pantalone.

The long first scene of Act Two gives us deeper insights into Volpone (Mosca, though present, is silent once Scoto's act begins); the rest of the act asks us to look more searchingly at Mosca's identity when he stands apart from his master. Mosca has been dispatched to Corvino's house to get Celia to visit Volpone without delay; he arrives to find Corvino still so determined not to be type-cast as Pantalone that he is planning preposterous safeguards for Celia's chastity ('thy restraint before was liberty / To what I now decree' II. v. 48–9). This is a real challenge to Mosca's powers of invention: he has to create a scenario in which Corvino will willingly play the one role he most dreads being cast as: the cuckold. First he takes Corvino's mind off Celia by exciting his jealousy of his rivals and making him doubt his perceptions and judgement: Mosca simply informs Corvino that Voltore and Corbaccio have revived the ailing Volpone with some of Scoto's elixir. He then flatters the husband's self-importance by stating that he has come straight to Corvino for help to resolve a dilemma: the College of Physicians has pronounced that the only lasting cure for Volpone 'was no other means / But some young woman must be straight sought out, / Lusty, and full of juice, to sleep by him' II. vi. 33–5). Again he touches on Corvino's jealousy of rival heirs ('they are all / Now striving who shall first present him' II. vi. 46–7); dismisses Corvino's first suggestion of a 'common Courtesan' as dangerous ('they are all so subtle, full of art . . . we may perchance / Light on a quean may cheat us all' II. vi. 52–5); then sits quietly by merely urging Corvino to 'think, think, think, think, think, think, sir' till Corvino proffers Celia. Greed gets the better of Corvino's sexual possessiveness. Moreover he is left supposing that he himself magnanimously on impulse devised the scenario that Mosca has artfully created for him. The tricking of Pantalone is a staple plot in *commedia* but the prototype lacks the psychological intricacies of Mosca's improvisation. The whole episode is a characteristic Jonsonian strategy: he takes a familiar dramatic situation and works it so that we, his theatre-audience, hanker excitedly for the known outcome, expecting that conclusion to be reached by an original twist in the plotting which will surprise and delight us. The twist here is both uproarious and shocking: Pantalone actually chooses to prostitute the wife he has so scrupulously guarded. And he is terribly pleased with himself at his decision: where he began the scene cursing Celia as the death of his honour, Corvino ends by showering her with kisses. Mosca has effected a transformation before our eyes that seemed against all odds. He has succeeded because he has the dramatist's penetrating insight into motive and into the nature and relative strengths of the various passions; his victims are helpless before that perception of their innermost selves.

We next see Mosca alone and he is beside himself with glee at this new exercise of his powers ('I could skip / Out of my skin now, like a subtle snake, / I am so limber!' III. i. 5–7) and he proves his mastery immediately with a show of crocodile tears that win over to his friendship the hostile and suspicious Bonario, Corbaccio's son. Mosca knows that emotions are fluctuating and therefore readily malleable, and so he delights in manipulating people's moods usually to the antitheses of those in which he finds them: first Corvino, then Bonario, and finally in this act Lady Would-Be (whom he discovers on his return to be amorously disposed towards Volpone but rapidly sends from the house a vengeful fury in the belief that, if she is quick, she will catch her husband *in flagrante* with 'the most cunning courtesan'). The wily slave of Roman comedy ravelled then resolved one intrigue to his satisfaction; Mosca possesses the Renaissance dramatist's skill at contriving, developing, interweaving a series of subplots involving not only the three original rival suitors but their dependents, a fourth suitor in Lady Would-Be and – a most daring stroke! – a character he has not yet even seen (Sir Politick). All the characters of the play are at his command to bend whichever way his will dictates. When Bonario stupidly anticipates his cue and intrudes unexpectedly into the scenario designed for Corvino and Celia, it proves less a catastrophe than the kind of complication a master craftsman throws in to prove his assured control of character and event. With breathtaking agility of mind Mosca manipulates everyone but the two Englishmen, Peregrine and Sir Politick, into a courtroom and, though he has to work hard, soon has everyone 'placed' as he wants them.

It is sometimes argued that Volpone is outstanding amongst the characters of the play for his intelligence, but it is Mosca who has the quicker wits and more flexible mind – creative, shrewd, worldly-wise. Yet the trial scene which he considers his masterpiece is a travesty of what should be the proper aim of imagination and of art. Mosca's scenario has brought out the worst in the three suitors, who now find themselves condemned to play publicly the caricatures they feared ever having to admit to being – Voltore the *bent* lawyer, Corbaccio the dotard-father and Corvino the self-confessed cuckold. Bonario and Celia, the only steadfast characters seemingly in Venice, are accused of being devious actors who have pretended to virtues the more conveniently to practise vice and intrigue: Bonario is denounced as 'Monster of men, swine, goat, wolf, parricide' (IV. v. 111) and Celia as 'a whore / Of most hot exercise' (IV. v. 17–18), a view that Lady Would-Be corroborates merely on hearsay of Mosca's telling. Volpone is summoned in to perform his act of dying before a large critical audience and surpasses himself with the verisimilitude of his mime (fear that he is playing for his life for once makes him identify wholly with his role to the point, we learn afterwards, when he imagined a sudden cramp was actually the palsy he was simulating). Mosca feeds Voltore with his lines and Voltore simply by adopting the voice and presence of authority quickly sways the Avocatori, the Venetian judges, to share his perception of things. This is black comedy of a very high order: the situation is profoundly shocking yet we cannot but admire Mosca's cool nerve and astute calculating in the face of crisis, the brazen effrontery of it all which is the key to his success, and the magnificent ingenuity. This is the first of Jonson's great comedies to be truly *dangerous* theatre, seducing us into complicity with what we know to be fundamentally immoral. But he does so, since his aim is 'to mix profit with [our] pleasure', to sharpen our powers of discrimination. Mosca's attributes – artistry, intellectual rigour, a daring imagination – are not in themselves vicious; we watch them becoming so in a grey, materialistic world where financial gain is the only means of achieving status or prestige. This artist is conditioned by the society he frequents and his art is an exact image of its perversity. But Mosca's insight is learned at the cost of his own corruption and the last laugh ironically is on him.

Where modern critics tend to admire the inexorability of Jonson's plotting in *Volpone*, their Restoration and eighteenth-century counterparts expressed reservations especially about the last act. John Dennis was not alone in finding there 'the greatest alteration . . . without any apparent cause. The design of *Volpone* is to Cheat, he has carried on a Cheat for three years together, with Cunning and with Success. And yet he on a sudden in cold blood does a thing, which he cannot but know must Endanger the ruining all'.[3] This line of criticism may grow out of a commonplace assumption that has long dogged appreciation of Jonson's artistry: that because he writes satirical comedy, he is more concerned with intricacies of plot than intricacies of character delineation and that in consequence his *dramatis personae* are two-dimensional caricatures that may develop in intensity but not psychological complexity. John Creaser and Anne Barton have recently persuasively argued otherwise.[4] Act Five is a perfectly logical development of the action if one has been attending to a number of psychological

nuances in what has gone before. We first encounter Volpone and
Mosca in Act Five resting in a state of euphoria and exhaustion
after the great *coup de théâtre* of the courtroom. Mosca, who
knows his place, interestingly talks of '*our* masterpiece' and opines
'We cannot think to go beyond this' (V. ii. 12–13). Volpone offers
a generous (but true) corrective: 'Thou hast played *thy* prize, my
precious Mosca'. Though Mosca speaks of their working together
as a team, he insinuates that Volpone was not a little frightened
by their recent brush with the law: ' 'T seemed to me you sweat,
sir' and 'But confess, sir / Were you not daunted?' (V. ii. 37 and
39). The deference makes the barb sharper: it implies that his is
the superior brain and nerve. Whatever Mosca's intention,
Volpone – his mind aflame with the 'lusty wine' he has been
imbibing since the start of the scene to quell the very nervousness
Mosca has detected – sees his parasite's tone as a challenge. When
Mosca muses that it is time Voltore and his rivals were finally
'cozen'd', Volpone sees his chance; without consulting Mosca he
issues commands and sets in motion a new device of his own
shaping. From the first we have noted tensions between master
and man and Volpone's anxiety to play alone without Mosca's
influence. Fine though his escapade as Scoto was, it ended in a
beating; by no means later could Volpone stay 'in character' and
either silence Lady Would-Be's tedious prattle or fend off her
solicitous petting while Mosca was absent. We have noted too
Volpone's liking for flamboyant gestures. His impetuosity now
does not bode well.

Master and man undergo the last of their transformations: at ✝
Volpone's command they become each other. Mosca dons the
robes of a magnifico to act in a scenario of Volpone's invention
and later, to further the action he has set going, Volpone disguises
himself as a servant of the court. Volpone has it given out that he
is dead; writes Mosca's name in his will; instructs the parasite to
sit and make an inventory of his 'inheritance'; and hides behind a
curtain to enjoy the spectacle of Voltore, Corbaccio and Corvino
discovering they have been cozened. Not content with watching
their initial shock and rage, he chooses to go after them to observe
more closely how bitterly they suffer. One by one he accosts them
in his humble *persona* as Sergeant of Law and solicitously enquires
after their well-being in a manner calculated to make their torture
worse. This scenario is decidedly nastier in tone than any Mosca

devised. Volpone shows no compassion for his dupes even though
he has made them what they are. The action gravitates to the
court again, ostensibly to hear judgement passed on Celia and
Bonario. Attempting to recover a little dignity and self-respect
Voltore and the others begin now to tell a different story, trying
to lay all the blame on Mosca; and Volpone takes advantage of
the general confusion to try to manipulate everyone present after
Mosca's fashion, giving them cues how to behave until the suitors
in particular act with a manic frenzy as if they were possessed.
But there is a marked difference: Mosca knew his characters
through and through and so could easily accommodate any
unexpected move they might chance to make. Volpone thinks he
has such supreme control and assumes that all his cast are
completely predictable; he quite forgets that his scenario has
liberated Mosca from his normally complying and subservient
function. Mosca determines to stay in his new role of magnifico.
Given a contest between the two of them, we can guess who will
be victor: Mosca has proved himself again and again the practised
expert at improvisation and performance; Volpone by comparison
is an amateur. But we know also from past action that Volpone
has an aristocratic temper. When he senses defeat and humiliation
are imminent, he 'uncases' and exposes everyone present for the
fools they are:

> I am Volpone, and this is my knave;
> > [*Pointing to* Mosca.]
> This [*To* Voltore], his own knave; this [*To* Corbaccio] avarice's
>   fool;
> This [*To* Corvino], a chimera of wittol, fool, and knave;
> And, reverend fathers, since we all can hope
> Nought but a sentence, let's not now despair it.   (V. xii. 89–93)

It is the ultimate in flamboyant gestures, and it costs Volpone
everything, including his own self-respect. From the first he
despised others as knaves; scorn was the stimulus for all his play-
acting; now he despises himself for being their equal. It is a heroic
impulse but the outcome is 'mortifying':

> Thou, Volpone, . . . our judgement on thee
> Is that thy substance all be straight confiscate

To the hospital of the *Incurabili*.
And since the most was gotten by imposture,
By feigning lame, gout, palsy, and such diseases,
Thou art to lie in prison, cramped with irons,
Till thou be'st sick and lame indeed.

(V. xii. 116–23)

This is a malicious judgement yet it has an undeniable poetic justice. Self will now be forcibly identified with role: Volpone will get what he wishes, though ironically not what he wants.

Throughout *Volpone* Jonson has used ideas of acting, play-writing, improvisation in a series of conceits to illuminate the nature of greed: how it gets a grip on the mind and transforms people into caricatures of their dignified selves, how it perverts and exploits even the highest faculties to its own ends, makes comic travesties of normal human relationships and a farce of the legal process. All the conscious theatricality gives a powerful and disturbing immediacy to the play in performance. The characters who inhabit the play-world that is the Venice of *Volpone* rapidly lose the power to distinguish between fiction and fact. Sanity, we see, lies in maintaining a rigorous detachment, but Volpone for one actually wishes to escape the burden of sustaining a responsible objectivity and actively seeks identification with a fictional role; he continues to yearn for that total abnegation of self-hood even when his efforts to achieve it result in painfully rude awakenings to his physical reality. Why he seeks that escape is made clear to us only in the moment of his 'uncasing' – a profound disgust for the whole human condition. What the complex meta-theatrical awareness with which Jonson enriches his play conveys is the extent to which acquisitiveness, greed, avarice are symptoms of a spiritual and metaphysical anxiety. Whether he is playing a bedridden ancient or Scoto of Manuta with his magical elixir, Volpone is confronting his audiences with images of the state to which they all must come as subject to time; but instead of learning from these portrayals in all humility, his audiences are goaded by them into shoring up more and more fragments of wealth against their ruin. The effect of Volpone's playing is anything but cathartic. In one of the richest jokes in Act One we see the virtually senile Corbaccio reinvigorated by the discovery that Volpone is apparently in a worse state of degeneration than himself:

> Excellent, excellent! sure I shall outlast him!
> This makes me young again, a score of years.
>
> (I. iv. 55–6)

The irony is that Volpone closes his mind to the darker intimations of his own art; he plays simply and cynically for material reward and for the pleasure of insulting his audiences; and, as he unconsciously admits in his seduction of Celia, he too longs for wealth to buy him transformation into the stuff of myth and legend. Jonson captures Volpone's whole intricate psychology in a felicitous pun when Volpone talks to Celia of his 'jovial plight': he seeks not one of Jove's many metamorphoses from a god to a beast, but the more hazardous translation from a brute to an immortal. Like Shakespeare's Richard II, Volpone plays in his person 'many parts' and all are expressions of a total discontent. His 'uncasing' calls an end to all the play-acting and punishment comes fast. To show as promptly as Volpone does the extent of the deceptions practised on the Avocatori is to expose their myopia and incapacity, so it is hardly surprising that their judgements are harsh. Volpone and the rest are condemned to live out their days in a full consciousness of their particular follies and their failure as social beings.

Just as the play seems over, Jonson produces a final unexpected flourish: Volpone bounds back free of his goalers, 'uncases' himself a second time to reveal the actor playing the role and speaks the epilogue requesting our applause. After all the games with costume, illusion and feigning that make up the plot of the play, it is a challenging (in some productions even disturbing) moment. What exactly will we be applauding: Volpone's devious skills or the actor's artistry in presenting those skills? Audiences invariably laugh at this dilemma, delighted at being so wittily tested by Jonson as to how alert the play has made them to intricate devices of trickery. He has dissolved the world of the play, restoring us to a sense of our immediate contingent reality but with a firm reminder that acting (and by now the idea of acting is carrying manifold resonances in our experience) is as insidiously a part of our world as of Volpone's Venice. By breaking all the illusion of his play-world, Jonson is ultimately flattering his audience's perceptions and judgement: he is showing us how, having a more detached relation to that play-world than the Avocatori and in consequence a more developed understanding of its condition, we can afford to be more generous in our response than they are. When we 'fare jovially' and clap our hands, it is an acknowledgement that Jonson has succeeded in his aim 'to mix profit with [our] pleasure'. Unlike Mosca who took possession of the minds and imagination of his victims in his scenarios, Jonson in his relation to us has been wholly creative: all his games with illusion are devised to illuminate and develop in us a rigorous discrimination by making us experience the dangers both of escapist art and of satire that is motivated only by contempt. Jonson's theatricality has a healthy purpose and Volpone's epilogue is proof of the sureness of his control.

That control was much disputed in the eighteenth century when *Volpone* was deemed too long, meandering and devoid of a proper unity of tone. The chief butts for criticism as farcical and irrelevant were the mountebank episode and the subplot involving Peregrine and Sir Politick. Yet cutting (a general practice in eighteenth-century performances) can have a disastrous effect on the working out of Jonson's strategies in the play. Volpone as mountebank adds immeasurably to our appreciation of Jonson's debate about the nature of acting and Sir Politick Would-Be serves an equally important function. As his name implies he longs to be thought sagacious and concerned for the well-being of the state yet his schemes to protect the Arsenal or keep Venice free of plague are preposterous beside the subtle corruptions that we see actively destroying the city. The inhabitants of Venice are suffering from a disease that afflicts the imagination and Sir Politick's own wayward fantasising is symptomatic. It is harmless enough at present though potentially dangerous in being rooted in a misplaced sense of self-importance; just such impulses to self-aggrandisement are what Mosca and Volpone work on to bring about the downfall of their various gulls, and Mosca is beginning to get a hold on Lady Would-Be. Peregrine for a while stands clear of the prevailing madness but, once he is implicated in its antic behaviour when suspected by Lady Would-Be of being a woman in disguise, he quickly succumbs to wilful impersonation. Seeking revenge on Sir Politick, Peregrine pretends to take Would-Be's dabbling in statecraft seriously; he comes heavily disguised and spins a yarn about Peregrine being a spy who has informed on Would-Be to the Senate, who have sent out a warrant for the Englishman's arrest. Touched on his weak spot, Sir Politick is totally taken in by Peregrine's earnestness: this is the dark side of being an important man of affairs, which he is suitably prepared for, having an 'engine . . . Fitted for these extremities' at the ready. He will simulate a tortoise inside a giant shell and escape detection. The device is the more bizarre for being premeditated and not impromptu. Discovered by the 'guard', his disguise quickly penetrated ('God so, he has garters!' – 'Aye, and gloves'. – 'Is this / Your fearful tortoise?' V. iv 73–4), Sir Politick has to suffer the further humiliation of discovering it is all Peregrine's joke at his expense. This 'uncasing' is wholly farcical, a simple exposure and castigating of folly, but it instils in the audience the sense of an imminent ending to the main action and prepares them to attend to the more complex significance of Volpone's unmasking. At all points the subplot has such affinities with the main action, though the treatment is invariably lighter in tone. I noted earlier that there is no precise exposition in the play to explain how Volpone and Mosca came to start their grand scheme. In the subplot we watch Peregrine first bemused, then irritated, and finally so angered by human folly that he takes revenge on it by devising a trick in the form of a play with disguises which shows Sir Politick the extent of his own stupidity. The revenge satisfies Peregrine's sense of injured dignity by demonstrating his superior wits. When the text of *Volpone* is acted in full, one is given a strong impression by the pattern of sophisticated parallels between the two plots and the carefully sustained contrast in tone that the impulse that moves Peregrine to berate Sir Politick is precisely that which three years ago set Volpone going on a venture where easy success has led him to exploit folly now at far darker levels of the psyche. The falcon after all like the fox is a creature that survives by preying.

A good director must enhance an audience's perception of this subtle network of patterns in the action if the fierce implacability that Yeats admired in *Volpone* is to be fully appreciated. The history of the play in performance this century is not a wholly gratifying one.[5] Individual episodes have usually impressed more than overall productions and there has been a marked tendency to sanitise Jonson's comedy: few actors have been encouraged to tap the deepening misanthropic disgust that motivates Volpone. The self-conscious theatricality of the text has been exploited at some stage of most productions, but it has rarely been made an organic creative principle controlling the shaping and invention of a performance. Sir Donald Wolfit's magnetic stage personality made him an ideal Volpone (1938 and 1940): he found a sensual relish in the character's success as an actor and his own actor-manager's *hauteur* made for a believable aristocratic extravagance of temper, tone and gesture; evil was a luxury to this Volpone, and never more so than when mesmerising Celia to utter helplessness. Aspects of Wolfit's temperament matched Jonson's conception superbly, other facets proved somewhat detrimental: centring the focus so strongly on his own performance meant that the all-important relationship with Mosca lacked complexity and tension so the last act had little sense of a manic race for the spoils.

Sir Ralph Richardson disappointed as Volpone (Memorial Theatre, Stratford-upon-Avon, 1952) for want, surprisingly, of imaginative fire and vehemence; he was decent, civilised rather than rapacious for gold, praise, sexual success. What critics found most perverse was Richardson's decision (against all indications in the text) to portray Volpone as an elderly man. A reading of the prompt copy for this production shows that it was not entirely devoid of felicitous insights: George Devine, who was always attentive to the theatrical realisation of the precise form of a play, directed with an eye chiefly to the comic or ironic possibilities of patterns of movement. When, for example, Lady Would-Be's arrival was announced to Volpone, he hid beneath the bedclothes; dismissing her servants, she immediately leapt on to the bed, took his hand, felt his heart while reeling off her recipes for medicine ('Seed-pearl were good now, boil'd with syrup of apples' III. iv. 52), grabbed his other hand when he remonstrated against her attentions, stroked his thigh on urging him to 'laugh and be lusty', then fell back prone beside him while reminiscing about 'the one sole man in all the world' with whom she could e'er sympathise. The bold licentiousness of Lady Would-Be was not only hilarious in itself, her movements anticipated many of Volpone's own in his seduction of Celia, thereby enhancing an audience's awareness of the brutal intent that lies behind his dulcet rhetoric long before frustration makes him openly aggressive.

Tyrone Guthrie's production for the National Theatre with Colin

Blakely (Old Vic, 1968) was an interesting experiment in that he chose to exploit the associations evoked by the characters' names. The cast studied appropriate animals and birds in London Zoo and aided by furred and feathered costumes, snouts and beaks, improvised expertly the characteristic movements and calls of crow, vulture, fox, parrot and so on. One admired the actors' skill but it was of a kind that totally undermined their capacity for character portrayal and they were compelled in consequence to invent more and more elaborate 'business' to sustain audience interest at the expense of Jonson's language. Moreover the actors were wearing such fantastic get-ups that nothing could be achieved symbolically with the themes of disguise and impersonation. There was so much obvious acting going on that Jonson's strategies with the play disappeared from view.

Peter Hall, always masterly in his pacing of a production, got a wonderfully accelerating tempo from his cast (Olivier Theatre, 1977) that paused only for a rapturous seduction scene: time seemed to stand still as if Celia's beauty brought Volpone (Paul Scofield) the vision of a wholly different world which he entered in excited reverie till her fear and his lust brought him back to an urgent reality. It was a finely conceived scene that gave poignant motivation to Volpone's subsequent behaviour which grows increasingly bitter and reckless. What detracted from the sensitivity of this approach to the play was John Bury's spare, clinically precise setting: three elegant arches, that were fitted out with green or white doors for various interiors, spanned a marble floor patterned in concentric circles. This was a far cry from the Venice evoked by Jonson's text, a place of mess and decay, rats, sprats and urine. Had that Venice been realised on-stage, it would have made the obsessive drive of the characters and the transformation in Volpone effected by Celia more potent.

Far better was the setting for Bill Alexander's production for the Royal Shakespeare Company (The Other Place, 1983): an austere façade opened up into tiers of cupboards, doorways, windows that were filled at the start of the play with fusty documents, darkly gleaming jewels and plate; centre-stage was a large square rostrum, that became by turns Volpone's bed, Scoto's stall, the Judges' bench. This production did full justice to Jonson's self-conscious theatricality: Volpone possessed an elaborate make-up kit (described in the prop list as 'containing white gunge, green slime and gauze pad tinctured with lake and damp cloth'); we watched him expertly transform his face, don night-clothes and subside under a fox-fur coverlet; with the arrival of each new suitor he refreshed the face-painting, getting increasingly senile until Corvino's exit when he wiped the whole lurid mask away as he leapt from the bed. The rostrum became a stage-within-the-stage but not in any restrictive way; once the theatre-image was visually established in the audience's minds, some cunning variations were effected. When Corvino dragged Celia into Volpone's bedchamber and husband and wife began arguing about the ethics of her being there, they became so engrossed in their battle of wills (played very physically with Celia lying rigid on the floor and Corvino trying forcibly to shift her) that they were oblivious of the fact that Mosca and Volpone, clutching each other to stifle their laughter, were sitting together watching the antics of the couple like spectators at a farce. Time and again we were made conscious like this of our own immediate role in the theatre as audience as if to have us question the tenor of our response. Other notable instances were during Celia's seduction when three windows silently opened to reveal Nano, Androgyno and Castrone taking a voyeuristic pleasure in the proceedings and in the trial when the Avocatori appeared ranked on the rostra directly facing us and looking down on the bizarre show being enacted for them to interpret and resolve. A due weight of attention was given to the subplot and time was carefully taken as each new set of characters entered the action to show how in particular they manifested the prevailing disease of wanting to be other than what they patently were. (Lady Would-Be, in a nice interpretation of her name, was clearly *nouveau-riche*, betraying in moments of tension her Cockney origins.) Only Celia and Bonario were content simply to *be* and resisted the temptation to try and become someone other; their passivity in consequence had a sound psychological base. By scrupulously staging Jonson's theatrical strategies, Bill Alexander found great richness of detail in *Volpone* that continually enhanced rather than detracted from the surface comedy. It was at once hilarious and profound, assured and metaphysical in its exploration of why humanity is so obsessed by the urge to act. Alexander's was the proper approach to Jonson.

5
'Epicoene'

In introducing his edition of the play L. A. Beaurline expresses the
hope that 'with our recent interest in Pirandello and Giraudoux's
theater of pretense and illusion . . . some enterprising directors
will restore *Epicoene* to its rightful place in the dramatic repertory'.[1]
Pinter in *The Lover* and *Old Times* and Orton in *What The Butler
Saw* have come even closer to the spirit and subject-matter of
Jonson's comedy and yet the strategies that motivate their games
with illusion and pretence are fundamentally different from Jonson's. They rely on present-day audiences' acceptance of the
conventions of fourth-wall realism and an inherited mode of
characterisation centred on a belief in what D. H. Lawrence called
the 'stable ego'; Jonson played tricks with his contemporary
audience's acceptance of the highly stylised conventions of a troupe
of child-actors (the Children of the Queen's Revels at Whitefriars)
and a long-standing tradition of female roles *always* being played
by boys or young men. To judge by the roles written for such
performers the art was far more subtle even in comedy than that
of transvestite or 'drag' acts in the modern theatre. Today one is
consciously aware of *difference*, however clever the impersonation,
aware in fact of the artistry, the ingenuity involved. The nearest
we can perhaps approach the convention of Jonson's day is in the
onnagata of Japanese theatre where the female impersonator is
one element in a totally stylised performance and one's acceptance
of the illusion is complete. When the National Theatre in 1967
staged *As You Like It* with an all-male cast, there was no suggestion

of caricature about the playing of Rosalind or Celia but one watched the performance mindful always that the conventions being set up for this particular production were experimental and innovatory: they were remarkable and we had to adjust to them imaginatively; we did not take them for granted as Shakespeare's original audience did. The fact of that self-consciousness about female impersonation in the modern theatre means that the major strategy of *Epicoene* can no longer work in the way it was devised to do.

When Dauphine pulls the wig off Epicoene in the final moments of the play and shows Morose that the marriage he despairs of is null and void since his partner is in actuality a boy, the incident must have been as disturbing for the audience as for the characters on-stage. This is the denouement Dauphine has worked for coolly and deviously. It is an 'uncasing' that is as startling as Volpone's but it is here a cunning design not an impulsive gesture and it leaves everyone in the play-world shocked and vulnerable. Dauphine's strategy, long prepared for and wholly secret, is also part of a greater strategy of Jonson's. His plot concerning Morose's marriage to Epicoene draws on two popular subjects: the man who weds a seemingly submissive woman only to discover she is a termagant or a shrew, and the man who is tricked into marrying a boy who has been dressed up as a girl. Traditionally in treatments of the second plot (which goes back at least as far as Plautus in *Casina*) the audience is let in on the hoax from the start, just as the audience is given good reasons why Viola and Rosalind choose to dress up as men. Jonson manipulates both these plots but artfully leads his audience to suppose until the climax that they are watching only a variation of the first. By the end of Act Three that plot has achieved its comic reversal: Epicoene, the apparently 'silent' woman, has found her voice ('You can speak then! . . . Oh immodesty! A manifest woman!' III. iv. 31 and 39) and Morose's house, until now a place of unnatural because enforced quiet, has been inundated with a rising tide of noise as more and more of her friends come to celebrate the bridal with feasting, music, trumpets and drums. Morose's antisocial behaviour (his pursuit in life of the silence and stillness of the grave) seems to have been fully explored and suitably castigated.

Act Four begins with a short reprise of Truewit's discourses on the necessary art for women of cosmetics and on fashionable modes of courtship between the sexes with which the play began and then shifts its focus decisively away from Morose and Epicoene on to the Otters, Daw, La Foole and the Collegiates. They all smugly contributed to Morose's undoing, now it is their turn to suffer at the hands of Truewit, Dauphine and Clerimont. The tone and quality of the humour in this act begins noticeably to change. Otter, who is painstakingly attentive to his wife's every whim in her presence, is egged on by the gallants to speak his mind about her when in private and in his cups, and they hide her in the room to overhear his abuse: a battle rapidly ensues between man and wife. This is still on the level of the vigorous horseplay that obtained in the bridal scenes and the humour derives from exploiting another stereotype of disastrous marriage. There is horseplay too in the trouncing of Daw and La Foole which follows but Truewit, who sets about exposing what cowards these braggarts are at heart, is growing more sophisticated in his trickery. He devises a scheme whereby Daw and La Foole suppose they have revealed their true selves only to each other and have stood correction (the one by being kicked, the other by having his nose tweaked) in utter privacy at the other's hands. In fact Dauphine with the aid of a disguise and a blindfold has actually administered the punishments and the proceedings have been witnessed from 'above' by Epicoene and the Collegiate ladies. The consequence of this is that Daw and La Foole, unaware of their public disgrace, continue to vaunt their braggart selves to the secret amusement of everyone else. Jonson seems to be drawing deliberate attention to the supersubtleties of the plotting. Truewit, excited by his skill at masterminding the whole business, becomes sarcastic and petulant when Clerimont offers to help him out:

> CLERIMONT: . . . I could hit of some things that thou wilt miss, and thou wilt say are good ones.
> TRUEWIT: I warrant you. I pray forbear, I'll leave it off else.
> (IV. v. 131–3)

He has a further trick up his sleeve. Watching Dauphine trounce Daw and La Foole, he suspects, will give the Collegiates a sadistic thrill, as indeed it does: fickle in their affections, they all three become instantly enamoured of Dauphine as the embodiment of real manliness. Truewit sees no need to scheme for their exposure:

they will show themselves in their true light of their own accord. And so it proves: within seconds, each contrives to come privately to Dauphine to arrange an assignation and disparage her rivals. Meanwhile Clerimont encourages Sir John Daw and La Foole to boast of their sexual conquests; it takes but little cajoling and waggish innuendo to persuade them to drop their false modesty and scruples ('We must not wound reputation' V. i. 62); in no time they are slyly insinuating they have sampled the favours of all the Collegiates and of Epicoene:

LA FOOLE: Sir John had her maidenhead, indeed.
DAW: Oh, it pleases him to say so, sir, but Sir Amorous knows what's what as well.   (V. i. 80–2)

So much for knightly chivalry!

The comedy has deepened from a farcical exploration of the perils of mismatching in marriage to a concern for what constitutes a proper sexual identity. This theme was already implicit in the Morose–Epicoene plot: he, under his father's instruction, believes that the highest form of self-development lies in cultivating the life within; there lies serenity and he is searching for a *silent* woman as a harmonious soul mate. Quiet self-sufficiency in women was the contemporary ideal. Sir Thomas Overbury a few years later was to describe *A Good Woman* as one who 'is much within, and frames outward things to her mind, not her mind to them. Shee weares good clothes but never better; for shee finds no degree beyond *decencie*. Shee hath a content of her owne, and so seekes not an husband, but finds him'. *A Good Wife*, he insists, is 'more seene than heard' since 'she leaves tattling to the gossips of the town': moreover, 'stubbornnesse and obstinacy are hearbs that grow not in her garden'.[2] Epicoene is perfection itself by these criteria. Yet how, if a woman is silent, do you gauge whether what lies within is all virtue? Morose studies Epicoene's appearance ('her temper of beauty has the true height of my blood' II. v. 19), then questions her about her views on what poses fashionably for dalliance and coquetry and about her attitude to dress. In all things she defers to his judgement. Within seconds of being his wife, however, she begins stridently to assert her own opinions, showing no regard for her husband's values or susceptibilities whatever. Her submissiveness during Morose's courtship was all a con-trick, no more than artful (and wholly persuasive) acting. But is the virago that finds release after the wedding any more typical of the quintessentially feminine than the dutiful mouse?

The portrait of the Otters' marriage approaches the same issue from a masculine perspective. Mrs Otter is the wealthier partner and she controls her husband's finances so as to compel him to flatter her with his attentions in public to get his livelihood: he is paid to act the role of solicitous husband. Here is another perversion of a fashionable amatory ideal: courtly lady pursued by her devoted servant-lover. However, Mrs Otter is a business-woman and one who is in no way magnanimously disposed; she expects her husband to adopt the manners of a literal servant and accordingly dresses him as one. The whole charade is designed to sustain her pretensions to being an aristocrat: his 'Princess'. She even resents it when in private he tries to live out a more acceptably masculine image of himself as jolly roisterer with a passion (and a giant capacity) for drink. Traditional stereotypes of bullying wife and hen-pecked spouse they may be, but Jonson has taken care to give them a social and psychological complexity that reinvigorates the convention even while extending his exploration of the state of matrimony as more a matter of role-playing than of trust and integrity. Significantly we first encounter the Otters when they suppose themselves wholly private and unobserved, so she is at her most imperious and he rebellious, being by turns wheedling or resentful. We know they are being covertly watched by Truewit, Clerimont and Dauphine; the moment she suspects the gallants are at hand, she insists they adopt their public *personae* ('Go to, behave yourself distinctly and with good morality, or I protest, I'll take away your exhibition' III. i. 51–3). There is a prompt transformation in them both. Yet which self, public or private, is the true one and which the acted role? By the time we meet them together again in Act Four the situation has become more intricate. Otter, relaxing with a group of male companions, begins under the influence of heavy drinking to project a bold self that he would ideally like to be on all occasions. He swaggers and speaks with increasing contempt of his wife; she is 'a cook, a laundress, a household drudge that serves my necessary turns' (IV. ii. 44–5) – all in actuality his functions in their household. Gaining confidence he probes deeper: she is 'without any good fashion or breeding: *mala bestia*' (IV. ii. 66–7). Up to a point this is true, but ironically

this was her view of him in their opening scene. Oblivious of the
fact that she is by now overhearing his every word, he betrays all
the most intimate details of her dressing-room: 'All her teeth were
made i' the Blackfriars, both her eyebrows in the Strand and her
hair in Silver Street. Every part o' the town owns a piece of
her. . . . She takes herself asunder still when she goes to bed into
some twenty boxes, and about next day noon is put together again,
like a great German clock' (IV. ii. 82–9). Everything in her
appearance is fake; nothing about her is natural. Again in some
measure this is true but voicing the matter is cruelly malicious;
and the judgement rebounds on him, proving him to be the boorish
oaf he is struggling to pretend that he is not. Instead of maintaining
a stoic dignity in the face of such detractions, Mrs Otter rushes
forth a veritable fury, insisting on her gentility even while soundly
buffeting her husband whom she has felled to the ground with the
sheer violence of her attack: 'Thou Judas, to offer to betray thy
Princess! I'll make thee an example –' (IV. ii. 105–6). Otter is
instantly a whimpering apologist. The more they insist on their
sexual identities, the more preposterous husband and wife become.
What in all this absurd behaviour can be said to be truly masculine
or feminine?

    As the last two acts progress character after character is revealed
as self-deluding and, sexually, a poseur. Everything that should
confer honour on a man – learning, courage, magnanimity in
friendship, a fastidious attention to one's own honour and that of
others, especially women – is shown to be either lacking in the
two knights, Daw and La Foole, or shallow in practice where it
should be a deep-grained habit. They may have a superficial sense
of style but both are effeminate asses. The three collegiate women,
Haughty, Centaur and Mavis, have separated from their husbands
and aspire to emulate men's independence of mind and spirit; they
seek freedom from the conventional patterns of ideal womanhood.
In practice what they seek is a less attractive aspect of masculine
freedom – the opportunity to go philandering. The very first
exchange in the play between Clerimont and his page informs us
that Lady Haughty, principal of their college, is so insatiable that
she will assault even a young boy. All three are stirred by
Dauphine's show of violence in punishing Daw and La Foole and
are prepared to prostitute themselves to this macho idol. To judge
by the surviving plays from their repertory, the various boy

companies excelled at accurate satirical portraiture. Jonson's own plays for such troupes afford notable examples: the idle courtiers in *Cynthia's Revels* clearly demand playing as recognisable types and the Induction to that play also includes a witty sending-up of various sorts of theatregoers; *The Poetaster* would be the funnier if Horace and the rival poets were obvious portrayals of Jonson, Marston and Dekker; there are also recorded instances of the companies falling into disgrace when their accurate mimicry touched on sensitive contemporary political or legal matters.[3] This is not to suggest that the characters in *Epicoene* are modelled on actual individuals (there is no evidence that this is so), rather it is to draw attention to an aspect of his players' artistry that Jonson chose increasingly to exploit as his play reached its climax. All the characters discussed assert an individuality but are proved like Epicoene and the Otters to be comic stereotypes at heart: Daw and La Foole, for all the intellectual pretensions of the one and the social pretensions of the other, are essentially versions of the *miles gloriosus*, loud in self-praise but ineffectual in action; and the three Collegiates are types of the rampant harridan, a regular butt in farce since Aristophanes' day. A remark of Jonson's in the dedication of his next play, *The Alchemist*, to Lady Wroth illuminates his dramatic tactics here: he denies himself the pleasure of protesting her excellences at too great a length lest he should seem 'like one of the ambitious faces of the time: who, the more they paint, are the less themselves'.[4] Jonson in *Epicoene* is drawing a distinction between the conventional and the stereotypical as if to question what is *normal* male and female behaviour.

Conventions define normality in terms of what is socially acceptable by a common consensus of opinion at a given point in time. Comic stereotypes in one way define aberrations from the norm yet, unlike caricatures, they do not refer to isolated, specific instances. Rather they are a recognition of a constant and inevitable pattern of deviation. They constitute a kind of alternative normality. Many comedies assert the *status quo* by requiring us to laugh at aberration, yet the recurrence of that strategy and of the stereotypes implies that aberration is a predictable consequence of creating conventions. The conventional norms in the case of sexual behaviour are highly restrictive and the aberrations that give rise to comic stereotypes inevitably involve a blurring of the boundaries that distinguish male from female. The women in the play all ape the tones, mannerisms and energy normally deemed masculine attributes, while Morose, Otter, Daw and La Foole become passive, submissive, outwardly faint-hearted (even if inwardly rebellious). In its way Morose's pursuit through life of a studied silence is the epitome of what Overbury for one thought best in women. We have reached a point by the middle of Act Five where sheer anarchy threatens to prevail; this is a situation one would expect in a good comedy or farce, but in *Epicoene*, as the very title of the play intimates, it is anarchy of a peculiarly intimate kind, involving resistance to traditional definitions of gender. It is a dilemma that Jonson's dramatic method makes an audience share. The colourful characters with the richest comic potential are the ones who strike out an individual path against the prevailing conventions: they provide the substance of the drama. Normality in the play is represented by the three gallants and yet they are an oddly lacklustre trio: they share an attitude of confident superiority; Truewit is distinguishable by his volubility and his capacity for a seemingly endless invention of horseplay; Dauphine is remarkable for a streak of callousness; but they all are in want of real personality. (Though Colley Cibber was consoling himself in 1700 for not getting the major role of Truewit that he coveted, he was right to criticise the character's 'dry Enterprises and busy Conduct'; Daw, the role he did play, does offer an actor more opportunities for interpretation, with what Cibber called his 'coxcombly follies'.[5]) Throughout the play Truewit has manipulated the other characters into acting scenes in which they have revealed their most intimate and vulnerable selves and he has done this for the sheer hell of it and to entertain his two friends. Jonson often places an audience on-stage whose visible responses cause the theatre audience to look more closely at their own. Here he offers a parade of traditional comic stereotypes relating to marriage and sexuality yet in each case provides them with a degree of psychological complexity that makes them more than stock figures treated in a routine fashion. The representatives of normality on-stage, Truewit, Dauphine and Clerimont, laugh long and laugh heartlessly at what is clearly to them no more than a freak-show, a series of grotesques whom they will put through their paces with cruel relish. If this is the conventional response to such stereotypes, then the normal is at a far remove from the proper.

It is at this point that Jonson unexpectedly turns our attention back to Morose and Epicoene. We may have supposed that their story was ended and that they had been suitably *placed*, but we have not been allowed to forget them. Morose has made several sallies into the action of Act Four whenever the noise level has reached a pitch that has penetrated through to the roof where he has hidden himself away under a mountain of nightcaps to block his hearing. On each occasion the gallants have calmed him down with mock solicitude. Epicoene we see being educated by the Collegiates in the ways of independence: one's status as wife, they inform her, is defined entirely by one's possessions – coach and four horses, woman, chambermaid, page, gentleman-usher, French cook and four grooms; as for a husband, he exists merely as a means to prove one's superior strengths ('Here's Centaur has immortaliz'd herself with taming of her wild male' IV. iii. 25–6). These brief episodes are merely amplifying the view we have of husband and wife that Jonson established by the end of Act Three. Truewit, having gone through the list of available persons to mock but by now positively teeming with inspiration, decides to go to work even more savagely on Morose. By feigning sympathy for Morose's plight, the gallants have discovered the old man's desperation to annul his marriage at any price. Truewit disguises Otter and Cutbeard as lawyers and instructs them to debate the various grounds for divorce; they are alternately to excite and dash his hopes. Morose has found he has cast himself in the role of a fool by his own malice and impetuosity (his only motive in marrying was to beget an heir and disinherit his nephew Dauphine, whom he despises); his anxiety now is to resist that demeaning label on his identity. Yet, as the lawyers pursue their lecture, Morose discovers he can only escape one restricting stereotype by embracing another: impotent old man, madman or ('worst of all worst worsts that hell could have devis'd' V. iv. 132) cuckold – each the butt of farcical laughter. It is here that Dauphine offers Morose release in return for his uncle's inheritance and 'uncases' Epicoene. Morose, pushed by despair to the most abject of levels, had even been willing to declare 'I am no man, ladies' (V. iv. 40); now Dauphine shows Epicoene to be no woman. Epicoene is a boy, a child-actor cleverly trained.

The characters on-stage are stupefied by the revelation: Morose has his freedom but his gullibility is reconfirmed; the Collegiates find they have confessed their innermost secrets to a man; Daw and La Foole are shown to be liars in claiming to have slept with Epicoene and had her maidenhead; and Clerimont and Truewit are shocked at the deviousness of their supposed friend, Dauphine, in sharing with them no part of his scheme. Dauphine stands revealed as a cold-blooded opportunist who has got what he wanted financially (Morose's whole estate) with no scruples about the possible consequences to his reputation. What of Jonson's audience? The more ardent theatregoers must have recognised that there is a second version of the plot of the old man who marries a shrew in which the wife is known to be a man in disguise and have laughed at Jonson's tricking them. The moment must have been more startling for the majority, for Jonson has torn apart the whole fabric of illusion on which the art of performance in their theatre rested. In one sense they had known all along that Epicoene was a boy in skirts: it was an accepted dramatic convention of the day regarding the playing of all female roles and one taken so completely on trust that disbelief was quite suspended. If it is an acceptable social practice in particular circumstances for boys to become women to the delight and edification of everyone present, how can we in all integrity make prescriptions about what constitutes a proper normality in gender-relations and sexual behaviour? Values in Jonson's mature comedies are usually conspicuous by their absence: all the relationships in the play – marriages, friendships – have by this conclusion been shown to be wanting in generosity and trust. They are the qualities most noticeably absent from the dealings of the three gallants, who see themselves as the most dashing embodiments of masculinity in the play and as models of perfection where civilised manners are concerned. The audiences at the private theatres where the boys' companies performed were predominantly middle and upper class, and male. A strategy that recurs in the best plays written for these theatres involves apparently flattering chauvinist, even at times misogynist, attitudes at first which then in the fullness of time are shown to be heartless and self-regarding. (Marston's *The Fawn* is a notable example, where most of the male characters end the play condemned to a life aboard a Ship of Fools.) Jonson's final game in *Epicoene* with the structures of realism and illusion seems similarly designed to appeal for compassion by making an audience question the grounds for its recurrent delight in comic sexual stereotypes.

Is the motive to show one's superiority or to express one's understanding and magnanimity? Which response is the better proof that one's own sexual identity is secure? After the writing of *Epicoene* Jonson's attitude to the characters in his plays becomes noticeably more expansive.

The climactic act of *Epicoene*, shocking the better to liberate, relied for its effectiveness on the precise working conditions of the company for which it was composed. The stage history of the play is instructive. If Drummond of Hawthornden is to be believed, 'ther was never one man [amongst its Jacobean audience] to say Plaudite to it',[6] presumably because it touched too many raw nerves; and it received but the one performance. It was revived for a single performance at Charles's court in 1636 and was the first of Jonson's comedies to be staged at the Restoration. Pepys thought it 'an excellent play' and relished the opportunities it afforded Kinaston, the celebrated boy actor, 'to appear in three shapes: first, as a poor woman in ordinary clothes, to please Morose; then in fine clothes, as a gallant, and in them was clearly the prettiest woman in the whole house, and lastly, as a man; and then likewise did appear the handsomest man in the house'.[7] Pepys clearly saw the play under ideal conditions, but though the popularity of *Epicoene* continued until the mid eighteenth century, it underwent a sea change once actresses after 1663 began to claim the right to appear in the title role. This made a nonsense of Jonson's strategies: he juggled with levels of theatrical artifice to come at a moment of truth; for Dauphine to uncase an Epicoene who was clearly an actress *en travestie* and claim she was a boy was to end the play in total confusion. As if troubled by the manifest absurdity of this, Colman revised the play and restructured it so that Epicoene's assumption of a will of her own and a stentorian voice with which to express it was delayed until far later in the action than in the original. This gave the actress considerable opportunities for comic mimed business and made it seem as if her transformation to a shrew was under the instruction of the Collegiates rather than a deliberate ploy of Dauphine's. Making Epicoene's transformation the climax of the action considerably softened the impact of the ending (Colman's was altogether a more amiable play than Jonson's) but that left the impression that the play was endorsing the sexual stereotypes that Jonson was choosing rather to question and explore. Though superficially sunnier in tone than Jonson's *Epicoene*, Colman's version is actually less liberated.[8]

Revivals in the twentieth century have been few; one of the most notable was at the York Festival in 1984 when Epicoene was played by a young man. The director took advantage of the contemporary fashion for unisex styles in hair and clothing: when Dauphine pulled off this Epicoene's wig, the actor's appearance remained totally unchanged, since his own locks were of an identical length, colour and texture with the wig. This was a bold invention with some of the sexual charge of Jonson's conceit, but it bore no relation to current conventions of performance so the moment could not have the absolute completeness of relevance to every level of the play's meaning in the theatre that Jonson envisaged.

Exploiting the looks of an actor with decidedly androgynous appeal like this is, perhaps, the nearest one can approximate today to the complexity of Jonson's ending. This line of argument was substantiated by the shortcomings of Danny Boyle's production of the play for the RSC (Swan Theatre, 1989) in which Epicoene, perversely, was given to an actor, John Hannah, whose face, gait, firm baritone timbres and Scottish accent proclaimed him obviously *male* from the outset. The effect was to throw the whole play off balance. The audience sensed instantly on this Epicoene's appearance that some trick was being played (though the identity of the chief perpetrator remained secret until the last) and that kept them superior to the stage-world throughout; they *awaited* a showdown and an unmasking; worse, it made everyone else in the play seem stupid for not seeing through so transparent a ruse. This was to miss a whole dimension of Jonson's play in which the audience themselves become implicated in his debate about sexual norms and conventions. Here we all sat amused and comfortably detached – the very attitudes Jonson's strategies are designed to unsettle. Boyle's production gave us no option but that superior response: he played safe by engaging with only the surface, the situational level, of the comedy rather than with its challenging implications.

Boyle's casting in many of the roles was far from ideal (chiefly because most of the actors, the women especially, were too young for the parts assigned them); several performances were superb, however, and the contrast afforded some insight into the demands made by Jonson of his actors. The Collegiates, for example, were without exception disappointing for being too obviously played as Jacobean progenitors of the pantomime dame yet absurdly by very young actresses for whom it was a genial romp; they are described as assuming a 'most masculine, or rather hermaphroditical authority' (I. i. 76) but the rich comic potential of this was virtually ignored. How misguided the chosen approach was is best exemplified by the portrayal of Madame Haughty, their president: we are told she possesses an appearance both 'grave and youthful' with 'her autumnal face, her piec'd beauty' (I. i. 79–80), while her *friend*, Centaur, is more precise in depicting her as one who, being 'above fifty', now 'pargets' (V. ii. 32–3). Amanda Bellamy in the role made no attempt to disguise her own natural good looks and mustered an arch soubrette charm where Jonson's text invites a much more complex creation: Haughty is a middle-aged virago who nonetheless by subtle artifice exudes an eerie, seductive allure (she has trapped Clerimont successfully in her toils to the point where he is utterly obsessed with her despite being appalled at what he knows is just clever contrivance). Hers is a triumph of the rampant will over all the physical odds against her. It is essential to Jonson's strategies in the play that characters like Haughty whom we think we can *place* as predictable should continually take us by surprise; and that requires sophisticated, not broad acting.

That experienced actors work best in Jonson was proved by a handful of performances which really took wing. Richard McCabe had previously played Tipto in *The New Inn* at the Swan in 1987; as Truewit he produced an intricate study of a man whose brain teems with inventions to keep at bay a fundamentally cynical vision of the world. He paced and coloured (one is tempted to write 'orchestrated') the character's vast speeches to show how once ideas possessed Truewit's imagination they took on a manic momentum pursuing their flight through breathtaking verbal arabesques in which he suddenly paused in awed surprise when the rush of words spontaneously evolved an image or perception that challenged his deep-rooted disgust with the world he inhabits. Here was a man alarmed by his own potential seriousness, for whom prattle was an escape from disquieting levels of insight. McCabe had such a command of the part that he effortlessly conveyed the illusion that it was all magnificently improvised.

David Bradley as Morose, the lover of quiet who quests for a silent wife because 'all discourses but mine own afflict me' (II. i. 3–4), had a fine sense of the ironies shaping the role. Absurd Morose may be in believing that rigidly preserving silence is the best way of cultivating the life of the mind, but he alone in the play sees the need to develop an inner being and this gives him a degree of dignity and stature that survives his becoming the butt of everyone else's ridicule. Bradley has an engaging quality of stillness as an actor; his movements are spare but exact. That style in performance here served to make Morose instantly a judgement on the popinjay society that surrounds him, which is why they attack him so mercilessly. The irony is that their attack reveals that his vaunted serenity is not all-consuming since he inhabits only the idea not the fact; as his name implies, his essential nature is shaped by hatred and malice towards others. He seeks silence in flight from a fierce anger. Bradley found a logic that gave due expression to all the extremes of Morose's temperament and with admirable skill kept the malevolence and desperation in the role within the bounds of comedy. He and McCabe played as perfect foils to each other, showing how their characters are subtly contrasting studies of malcontented souls; their many scenes together were exemplary of the proper art of acting in high comedy that was a joy to experience because both men clearly relished Jonson's text for the opportunities it afforded them for deft psychological portraiture. It is to be lamented that Boyle did not have the courage or the creative stamina to let the spirit evident in these episodes suffuse the play in its entirety. Had he done so, fewer reviewers might have been tempted to dismiss *Epicoene* as simply a black, misanthropic farce when it is a highly sophisticated comedy of manners. *Epicoene* is a finer play than Boyle's account of it suggested; but the major weakness of the production – the central portrayal of Epicoene – served only to strengthen the conviction that the greatness of this particular comedy is entirely circumscribed within the theatrical conditions for which it was originally written.

6
'The Alchemist'

Jonson the realist used his prologue to *Every Man In His Humour* to deal a blow at conventional Elizabethan stage-practice:

> To make a child, now swaddled, to proceed
> Man, and then shoot up, in one beard, and weed,
> Past threescore years: or, with three rusty swords,
> And help of some few foot-and-half-foot words,
> Fight over York and Lancaster's long jars:
> And in the tiring-house bring wounds to scars.

And he goes on to list numerous devices of illusion ('roll'd bullet heard / To say, it thunders'). He is questioning the validity of plays that need to establish principles of stylisation. Pushed to a logical extreme that line of argument would begin to question the very nature of drama as an exercise of the imagination requiring a willing suspension of disbelief on the part of its audiences. There is one dramatic genre – farce – that actually makes the willing suspension of disbelief its subject: it becomes the characters' whole mode of being, the longing that their condition in time should be transcendently different. This is as true of Aristophanes exploring whether life would be significantly better if women were in supreme control in parliament or if Aeschylus could be resurrected from the grave to combat with his art the cynicism prevailing in Athens, as it is of Feydeau investigating his characters' quest for the perfect sexual experience. Farce is about dreams of realising the impossible: as Subtle observes of Sir Epicure Mammon in *The Alchemist*, 'If his dream last, he'll turn the age to gold' (I. iv. 29).[1] Farcical humour derives from the dramatist's juxtaposing of fantasy alongside an all-too-insistent reality and from the tenacious hold of the characters on their private dreams seemingly against all odds. When Feydeau's adulterous lovers finally get to their assignation in their chosen hotel, they continue to believe they are on the threshold of unimaginable raptures despite the tatty, impersonal bedroom, a flow of implausible interruptions from harassed or bewildered strangers and the massing of the *gendarmerie* in the lobby downstairs zealously scenting out vice. Equally funny is the way each of these flabby, middle-aged lechers, who imagines himself to be another Paris or a Romeo, can miraculously summon up the stamina and agility of an Olympic athlete the moment his idyll is actually threatened. This is partly to save face, and partly to keep open at any cost the possibility of realising the dream-self on some future occasion.

In farce, each character is an actor on the epic stage of his imagination who chooses wilfully to suspend awareness of the grey reality that prevails around him. Seeking identification with his role makes him a rank amateur; the professional, as we saw in Brainworm and Tiberius, keeps a studied detachment, a consciousness aware of the fact of performing and alert to his effect on his audience; this allows him to encompass an endless variety of roles, whereas the character in farce continually type-casts himself. In *The Alchemist* Jonson creates a structure that examines this distinction: a series of farcical characters each intent on realising a *better* self come in the clutches of a trio, consummate actors all, who in a mercantile age are choosing to sell illusion as a commodity. With the aid of a few tawdry props and appropriate foot-and-half-foot words they give their clients the chance to star in their various private scenarios – at a price, of course. Face, Dol and Subtle are cashing in on the fashionable belief that alchemy can manufacture the philosopher's stone and from it distil an elixir that will solve all human ills. Alchemy was the dream to end all dreams. Jonson draws and sustains throughout the play a brilliant conceit relating alchemy, the refining of base metals into purest gold, with acting (the transformation of humble mortals into heroes). Subtle's alchemical laboratory we never see (patently it does not even exist); instead we watch the effects of the trio simply talking to their clients about its potential. All the magic is in the power of their words to feed each client's imagination until it invents a brave new world to its own satisfaction. By making these moments of self-transcendence plays within the larger play-structure, each carefully staged and paced by Face or Subtle, Jonson cunningly transforms a superb social comedy about Jacobean London into a serious disquisition on the nature of theatre. He was never one to let his 'judging spectators' rise comfortably superior to the stage-action. Theatre is as much a house of illusions as Lovewit's house becomes when left in his butler's charge; to it come clients who pay for the privilege of letting actors and dramatists for 'two short hours' possess their imaginations. The conscious theatricality of *The Alchemist* seems designed as a strategy to make an audience look beyond their immediate enjoyment of the action and question the motive for their laughter and for deliberately seeking out Jonson's and his actors' arts. Is it for purposes of escapism (if so, there are manifest dangers in identifying with any of the characters on-stage) or to seek to fine-tune one's sense and sensibility? In the themes and the strategies that shape its dramatic method *The Alchemist* shows how the seductions of city life are such that one must be ever on the alert. Young Kastril, newly come to London and already aware of its temptations, has one last and particularly pressing need to voice when he is checking out Subtle's credentials as a possible mentor: 'But does he teach / Living by the wits, too?' (III. iv. 41–2). Asked of Face, the most brilliant and adaptable of shape-changers, this is gloriously naïve. Yet how is one to gain real knowledge of a world as intricately devious as the London of the play (short of learning the hard way by making an ass of oneself like Kastril) except it be to submit to Jonson's strategies with a good grace?

It is because poets and dramatists exert great power over people's imaginations that Plato chose to expel them from his Utopia: they would be dangerous in fostering disaffection. *The Alchemist* opens with Dol Common trying to stop a quarrel that has blown up between her colleagues Face and Subtle, who to her consternation have quite forgotten the terms of the league of amity between them and are roundly abusing each other at the tops of their voices. Crying out against their arrogance and stupidity, she finally gains silence when she appeals to them to 'Have yet some care of me, o' your *republic*' (I. i. 110). It is tempting to see this as a joke at Plato's expense, the strategies of the play being conceived as a defence of the comic poet against Plato's strictures. Plato's thinking about a rationally ordered, ideal society was subversive in its time, even if only hypothetical, since to conceive of a Utopia is to imply criticism of the prevailing political set-up; so there is a certain appropriateness in the naming of this alternative underworld establishment of three thieves after his great *Republic*, based as it is on the principles of respect for each other's skills and an equal sharing of all income accruing from their endeavours. If the allusion to Plato is intended, it would make this the first of a series of significant moral inversions.

The political implications of Dol's remark go reverberating through the play and gain weight by being reiterated through a pattern of variations. What motivates each of the gulls to come to the house is found in time to be a wish to improve his social standing. Their aspirations, modest at first, grow, sharpen, intensify under Face, Subtle or Dol's nurture. Dapper wishes for a familiar to help him win when he risks an odd bet at the races but quickly sees himself leaving his position as lawyer's clerk, when his 'unresistible luck' brings him 'enough to buy a barony' (III. iv. 59–60); instead he will become a kind of Lord of Misrule, taking the honoured chair at ordinaries, the toast of card-sharpers. Drugger just wants to attract customers to his tobacco shop but is egged on to imagine himself rising through his guild to become mayor and marrying into the gentry. Mammon, already a knight, aspires to be master of untold wealth, a great lord and a benefactor to society conferring honour and prosperity on all he favours. Dame Pliant aspires to a title; Kastril to be a fashionable rake-hell, a name in society. Ananias and Tribulation, the Anabaptists, ostensibly engaged in charitable works, warm to Subtle's flattery and make no denial of his supposition that they would use the philosopher's stone to redeem their political position (they are 'silenced Saints'), win aristocratic friends to strengthen their temporal power and, hope against hope, displace the Holy Roman Empire throughout Europe. Even Surly the gamester, Mammon's companion, who suspects the trio for what they are, disguises himself as a Spanish grandee when he seeks to gain entrance to the house, for all he sees himself as a pillar of commonsense and rectitude. Mammon's self-image inflates with his every appearance until, impassioned in Dol's arms, he is promising to show her off

as his consort at 'feasts and triumphs' in such dazzling array that
her fame will make 'Queens . . . look pale' while 'Nero's Poppaea
may be lost in story' (IV. i. 138, 144–5). Dol, with mock ingen-
uousness, asks a pertinent question:

> But in a monarchy, how will this be?
> The prince will soon take notice, and both seize
> You and your Stone, it being a wealth unfit
> For any private subject . . .
> O, but beware, sir! You may come to end
> The remnant of your days in a loathed prison . . .
>
> (IV. i. 147–50, 152–3)

At the root of all their dreams lies a longing for esteem, position,
conspicuous social success (except for Kastril who would prefer
notoriety). Jonson establishes the point with a rich humour at the
expense of the two Puritans when he has Subtle sympathise with
them over the relief they will soon experience in possessing the
Stone when they need no longer worship in a preposterous
fashion ('leave off to make / Long-winded exercises' III. ii. 53–4) or
cultivate singularly bizarre habits simply to draw attention to
themselves, such as railing against plays 'to please the
alderman / Whose daily custard you devour' (III. ii. 89–90) or
taking such affected names as 'Tribulation, Persecution, / Restraint,
Long-patience' (III. ii. 93–4). Tribulation does not demur, he
merely points out smugly that such 'inventions' have made the
brethren 'grow soon and *profitably* famous' (III. ii. 101).

Dol begins the play warning her partners of the danger threatening the common wealth and well-being of their private republic if
they indulge in 'civil war'. Steadily as the play advances social
disaffection in varying degrees is seen to be the impulse behind
the 'itch of the mind', as Face calls it, from which the gulls suffer.
Face, Dol and Subtle profit by these rebellious instincts by
cleverly stimulating the gulls' anarchic desires while managing
simultaneously to contain them. But there is no denying that the
fantasies of Dapper, Tribulation and Mammon would, if actually
realised, be criminal: the Utopian self can only be realised in
opposition to the prevailing *status quo*. Mammon ecstatically

envisages the corruption of all normal relations and behaviour to
flatter his ego:

> I'll ha' no bawds,
> But fathers and mothers – they will do it best,
> Best of all others. And my flatterers
> Shall be the pure and gravest of divines
> That I can get for money. My mere fools
> Eloquent burgesses . . .   (II. ii. 57–62)

Interestingly the imagined alternative self is in each case constructed out of a perverted idea of the privileges enjoyed by the
aristocracy. Dapper yearns for a life of recklessly confident
gambling; Drugger for the arranged marriage that will consolidate
his estate; Mammon for an insatiable appetite for sensual gratifi-
cations which he will offset by philanthropy and charitable deeds
to swell his good opinion of himself; Tribulation, a cunning
manipulator of his fellow brethren, longs for the chance to exercise
his real skills in statesmanship on an international scale; Surly for
the voice of authority that commands immediate respect; Kastril
for the right to be totally irresponsible, living in the whim of the
moment. The result in each case is a parody of the aristocratic
temper; all miss its true spirit by being obsessed with that temper
as merely an expression of wealth. Were any of them to have his
desire fulfilled the consequences socially would be disastrous: each
fantasy-self is an exposure and exact judgement on the inadequacies
of the dreamer. Much Jacobean city-comedy sets out to satirise
the pretensions of the rapidly augmenting ranks of *nouveaux-
riches*: *The Alchemist* has few rivals for the shrewdness and depth
of its social insight. The persons to whom Jonson dedicated his
plays on publication were always carefully and aptly chosen. Sir
Philip Sidney was ever held in esteem by Jonson as the epitome
of excellence in aristocratic virtues, one who was in every sense
of the word a *good* man in scrupulously fulfilling the responsibilities
of his position. It is fitting that *The Alchemist* with its depiction of
a fallen world of would-be aristocrats should be offered to the
'judgement (which is Sidney's)' of Lady Mary Wroth as 'most
deserving her name and blood'.[2]

It is worth making this point because modern directors have a
tendency to go for the preposterousness of these little men with

voluptuous minds and so miss the element of danger in the play
that makes for a much richer humour. The anarchy that generally
prevails in farce and comedy has here, as frequently in Aristophanes, precise political implications. All too frequently today
the sense of danger is confined to the threat of Lovewit's imminent
return to his house. The problem is that the crimes contemplated
or effected in the play are not deemed to be as heinous now as
they were in 1610, and certainly are not punished today as
rigorously as then. Dabbling in the black or occult arts, pimping
and prostitution, 'laundering gold' (forgery) whether termed 'coining' or 'casting', thieving (notice how Jonson keeps reminding us
just how much money the trio have stolen from their clients in the
space of a few hours), fraud, overdressing above one's station like
Face as a 'whoreson, upstart, apocryphal captain' or Dol as 'my
Lord Whats'hum's sister' in a velvet gown met, if proven, with
savage correction.[3] Too vigorous horseplay in the fight between
Face and Subtle which opens the play often in modern productions
obscures Dol's genuine alarm. It is much more than a breach of
the peace that she is afraid they will be accused of. Carting, the
pillory and mutilation is the best that they could hope for if the
truth about them were known; the worst outcome would be
hanging:

> Shall we go make
> A sort of sober, scurvy, precise neighbours,
> That scarce have smiled twice, sin' the king came in,
> A feast of laughter at our follies? – rascals
> Would run themselves from breath, to see me ride,
> Or you t'have but a hole to thrust your heads in,
> For which you should pay ear-rent?   (I. i. 163–9)

Her fear quickly sobers them down. When a modern director and
cast find a way of intimating this danger to an audience, the effect
is to give the clients' relentless visits to the house a positively
manic urgency and to make Face, Dol and Subtle's activities in
receiving them seem ever more brilliantly inventive: they *must* be
brilliant as a matter of survival.

   In *Volpone* and *Epicoene* Jonson had experimented with ways
of creating the illusion that the stage-action was at various
points a spur-of-the-moment improvisation by one or more of his

characters. Mosca and Truewit gave virtuoso performances; Face, Subtle and Dol are remarkable for working superbly as a troupe: playing against manifestly dangerous odds is a spur to their wits. They change roles and identities with a wonderfully slick precision, Face especially. Each assumption of a role, each transformation, is total, involving not only a change of costume and perhaps make-up or wig but significantly too a convincing change of voice and idiom (Jonson several times in the play has Face as Captain go unrecognised by a character accustomed to dealing with him in his personification as Lungs and he is deemed missing for weeks by the neighbours who are used to seeing him, clean-shaven, in his butler's livery as Jeremy). With each arrival, they check they are wearing the appropriate costumes, then decide which of them are to appear in this episode, on what cues and in what tone; the one who knows the new gull best (usually Face who acts as general intelligencer) gives a quick character-sketch as the *donnée* about which they will extemporise, then all three trust to their proven skill to play off their colleagues' inventions. The whole scheme is set-up in a flash even as they are making themselves ready:

SUBTLE:	Who is it, Dol?
DOL COMMON:	A fine young quodling.
FACE:	O,
	My lawyer's clerk, I lighted on last night,
	In Holborn, at the Dagger. He would have
	(I told you of him) a familiar
	To rifle with at horses, and win cups.
DOL COMMON:	O, let him in.
SUBTLE:	Stay. Who shall do't?
FACE:	Get you
	Your robes on. I will meet him, as going out.
DOL COMMON:	And what shall I do?
FACE:	
	Not be seen, away!
	[*Exit* DOL COMMON.]
	Seem you very reserv'd.
SUBTLE:	Enough. [*Exit.*]

FACE: God b' w' you, sir!
           I pray you, let him know that I was here.
           His name is Dapper. I would gladly have
           stayed, but –

                                              (I. i. 189–99)

And they go straight into their act for Dapper's benefit without
pause. The fact that this rapid exchange is all beautifully contained
within regular lines of verse adds to the speed of the preparations
if those lines are meticulously observed in performance: this is
living by the wits after a fashion Kastril could never hope to
emulate.

Their technique is dazzling as they shift effortlessly between
seven differently evolving scenarios, all running concurrently,
several by Act Three being developed simultaneously. At one
point this requires Face to perform a veritable *tour de force*: he
speaks in Lungs' voice through the keyhold to Sir Epicure waiting
without; in his own workaday tones *sotto voce* giving instructions
to Dol and Subtle; as the Captain advising the blindfolded Dapper
how to conduct himself through the ritual in which he is being
'purified' ready to meet his aunt, the Queen of Faery; and in
squeaking falsetto as one of the elves searching the clerk for
evidence of worldly pelf. He has scarcely left the stage in his
captain's outfit to dispose of Dapper in 'Fortune's privy lodgings'
than he is back on again with Mammon and metamorphosed into
Lungs. It is the mark of their success that their dupes return
relentlessly to the house keeping the trio's services in constant
demand. Generally in farce the accelerating intrigue calls on an
actor's versatility, stamina and resourcefulness to express his
character's mounting panic and desperation; Face, however,
thrives on the exhilaration of living at a pitch of attention in order
to keep events under his control. He and Subtle make a dreadful
gaffe with Surly when he appears in his Spanish garb and with
umbered face: they presume because they do not understand a
word he says that he cannot possibly understand them and proceed
jokingly to tell him that he is going to be robbed, even repeating
themselves slowly and at the tops of their voices, as is the English
way with uncomprehending foreigners:

SURLY: *Por dios, señores, muy linda casa!*

SUBTLE:	What says he?
FACE:	Praises the house, I think;
	I know no more but's action.
SUBTLE:	Yes, the *casa*,
	My precious Diego, will prove fair enough,
	To cozen you in. Do you mark? you shall
	Be cozened, Diego.
FACE:	Cozened, do you see?
	My worthy Donzel, cozened.
SURLY:	*Entiendo*.
SUBTLE:	Do you intend it? So do we, dear Don.
	Have you brought pistolets or portagues?
	(IV. iii. 34–42)

Subtle has his suspicions ('Slud, he does look too fat to be a Spaniard' (IV. iii. 28)) but defers to Face's judgement – unwisely as things turn out. When Surly, watching Subtle later trying to rifle his pockets, reveals who he really is by speaking in his own voice and in English ('Will you, Don Bawd, and Pickpurse? [*Knocking him down.*] How now! Reel you?' IV. vi. 26), Subtle is stupefied. Until now the gulls, once *known*, have been completely predictable; Surly throws him right off cue and he *dries*. But when Face is drawn to the action, he coolly appraises the situation: the priggish Surly is so enamoured of his importance in having at last got centre-stage where he can castigate the world at large for its moral shortcomings that his attention is focused only on the quality of his own performance. Face quietly goes out to return with a motley assortment of their gulls – Kastril, Drugger, Ananias – who proceed to contest Surly's right to the star role. Kastril questions his manhood ('Where is he? Which is he? He is a slave / Whate'er he is, and the son of a whore' IV. vii. 4–5); Drugger his moral probity; and Ananias the decorum of his costume ('Thou look'st like Antichrist, in that lewd hat' IV. vii. 55). They demolish all Surly's pretensions to authority and force him to quit the stage. Face has surpassed himself in sheer ingenuity and imaginative daring – and all, seemingly, *impromptu*.

Masterly strategies contrived by Jonson's characters often, as we have seen in *Volpone* and *Epicoene*, cover masterly strategies worked by Jonson himself on his audience. When Surly threatens to expose the trio to the authorities (and we know from the

opening scene what the consequences of that will be), the play is
well on its way to a conclusion. Dapper is in the final stages of his
initiation and has only temporarily been baulked of getting his
familiar by the inopportune arrival of other gulls at the house;
Drugger has served his turn and lured Dame Pliant into Face and
Subtle's clutches; the Anabaptists have bought and made an
inventory of the goods in the cellar down to the last andiron that
Mammon has brought there ready to transmute into gold when he
finally possesses the stone; by getting Tribulation to agree now to
sponsor some secret coining, the trio have an effective weapon
over the Brethren in the form of blackmail, should they subsequently turn nasty over the tricks played on them; Mammon has
been spurred on by Dol to a display of unbridled lust that is the
cue for Face and Subtle to fake an explosion supposedly of
the alchemical apparatus, since the philosopher's tone by time-
honoured repute can come into the hands only of men 'free from
mortal sin and very virgin' (II. ii. 99). It is difficult to see where
the play could go next when Surly arrives coveting the role of *deus
ex machina*. Yet there is no obvious sense of an impending
conclusion at this point and we are frankly relieved and delighted
when Surly gets expelled from the action after threatening to stop
all the fun. Played well, the scene invariably provokes applause
the instant the door slams shut on his indignant figure. Scarcely
have we and Face taken breath than Dol races in with the news
that Lovewit has come home. From the first this was always
accepted as the natural termination of the 'venture tripartite' and
all the shared knavery: Lovewit was the expected *deus ex machina*.
(Peter Womack has shown that the first performances of *The
Alchemist* coincided with the reopening of the London theatres as
safe public venues after a particularly long season of plague, so
initial audiences would have had throughout the play a pressing
sense of Lovewit's likely arrival at any moment to complicate or
resolve the action.[4]) Having had a false attempt at an ending, we
could now justifiably suppose that Lovewit will bring matters to a
brisk and efficient close. But Jonson is never one to pander to an
audience's expectation. Face, cool as ever, makes a prompt
decision, gives his colleagues a new set of cues ('Be silent: not a
word, if he call or knock', pack all the stolen goods, take ship to
Ratcliff and await instructions about dividing the booty) and begins
calmly to metamorphose himself into a shape we have not seen

him in before – all his Captain's beard 'must off' to make
him 'appear smooth Jeremy', Lovewit's butler (IV. vii. 119–131).
Jonson now just as coolly breaks all the rules of drama: he shifts
his scene outside the house, introduces a whole new set of
characters and starts what promises to be a fresh action. The
quality of improvisation seems suddenly to take over the whole
drama. In effect the last act works like a musical coda: a surprising
finale is achieved by a magnificent flourish of all the foregoing
themes.

We find Lovewit beset by his neighbours complaining about the
weird goings-on in his house:

LOVEWIT:	Has there been such resort, say you?
NEI. 1:	Daily, sir.
NEI. 2:	And nightly, too.
NEI. 3:	Ay, some as brave as lords.
NEI. 4:	Ladies and gentlewomen.
NEI. 5:	Citizen's wives.
NEI. 1:	And knights.
NEI. 6:	In coaches.
NEI. 2:	Yes, and oyster-women.
NEI. 1:	Beside other gallants.
NEI. 3:	Sailors' wives.
NEI. 4:	Tobacco-men.
NEI. 5:	Another Pimlico! (V. i. 1–6)

Again if the verse lines are respected in the delivery, the scene
has a hilarious pace, exactly capturing the rhythms of tittle-tattling
gossip. What emerges from it all for the bemused Lovewit is that
his good neighbours have seen and heard much but *know* little
with any factual accuracy. From chance occurrences their fertile
imaginations have bred the tallest of stories:

NEI. 6:	About
	Some three week's since I heard a doleful cry,
	As I sat up a-mending my wife's stockings.
	. . . Yes, sir, like unto a man
	That had been strangled an hour, and could not
	speak. (IV. i. 32–7)

Clearly humdrum lives like these have welcomed a little excitement. When Face appears as Jeremy he is the perfect servant,
quiet-voiced, solicitous, even a shade obsequious. This, we find,
is Face's habitual role in life and he plays it to perfection, but who
can vouch that Jeremy is Face's genuine identity, knowing (as we
do) that he is such a consummate actor? Perhaps in the past
Jeremy may have been the man's stable ego, but after his
translation to the likes of Captain Face that old self can only be
resumed as a role in future. This causes us to reflect on the identity
of Lovewit throughout what follows.

In the list of *dramatis personae*, in the argument and throughout
the text of the play, Lovewit is described as simply 'the master of
the house'; his precise social standing is never defined. Clearly he
is a gentleman and a householder, sufficiently wealthy to retire to
the country when plague carries off his wife. He has no title, yet
everyone immediately defers to him his whole manner
clearly implies respect is his due. Circumstances having compelled
Jeremy to tell his master the truth, Lovewit takes over control of
the situation. He manipulates the law more deftly than Dapper or
the Brethren could do to deny anyone's claims to the goods stowed
away in his house, displaces Drugger in marrying the widow,
commands with authority as Surly never could, and acts with a
prompt, nonchalant effrontery that fills Kastril with admiration.
He has the knack of winning the game, prizes and all, without the
help of any charm or familiar; though he lacks the philosopher's
stone, he has a golden tongue and a precious wit that makes him
master of every eventuality; and without any profession of zeal or
belief in special divine favour he conspicuously betters his condition
financially and emotionally to the dismay of Ananias, Tribulation
and Mammon. Jeremy is required to dispose of his two partners
with a minimum of fuss in return for keeping his job as butler.
Except that he tells us that he loves 'a teeming wit', Lovewit
remains a complete enigma to the last: the only certain facts about
him are his intelligence, efficiency and power and the means by
which these are expressed – his tone of voice, which is always
meticulously judged, incisive and exact, the product of a disciplined
mind. Imagination in him as in Face, Subtle and Dol, is directed
wholly and penetratingly at the matter in hand; fancy plays no
part in its workings. He vaunts no self-importance, suffers no
qualms of conscience, but succeeds by being rigorously impersonal,

by projecting not a character but the stance and vocal attributes of a type; an upper-class imperiousness, that will brook no denial. It is a typical Jonsonian joke that the *deus ex machina* who visits the benighted world of the play should possess all the qualities that the gulls severally aspire to, yet conspicuously not be a true aristocrat in spirit any more than they are. Lovewit's is a more studied version of the role-model than any of theirs but his observations have been single-mindedly directed at those features which are distinctively expressive of power. He may have a genial sense of humour, but he is quite ruthless.

Lovewit's arrival in Act Five brings a refreshing note of common-sense to the proceedings. His verse is regular, contained, precise. It startles us into realising that for the best part of the last three acts Jonson has been getting us to listen to sheer nonsense. The verse has shaped language into syntactical units that have given it the appearance of sense but it would be well nigh impossible to paraphrase much of the dialogue. Face and Subtle (and to a lesser extent Dol) are adept at mesmerising their clients with scientific, fey, occult and simply street-wise jargons which they use with the incantatory power of adepts in some mystic rite. It is not what is said but the manner in which it is said that compels assent from all but Surly, just as ultimately it is Lovewit's manner that compels assent when he sends everyone but Jeremy, Kastril and his sister packing back to their private abodes to nurse their injured vanity, anger and shame. Listening to Subtle and Mammon discourse happily about alchemical practice – 'Let the water in glass E. be filtered / And put into the gripe's egg. Lute him well; / And leave him closed *in balneo*' (II. iii. 39–41) – excites Surly's derision: all this conjuring with terms is 'somewhat like tricks o' the cards, to cheat a man / With charming' (Surly is a gamester so can recognise a con-trick when he sees one). It is all a matter of 'brave language' to him, like canting, an attempt to invest the flotsam and waste of existence ('piss and eggshells, women's terms, man's blood, / Hair o' the head, burnt clouts, chalk, merds and clay' II. iii. 194–5) with *value*.

Morose had been appalled by the triviality of social relations and retreated into silence the better to cultivate his inner resources. Absurd though this mania is, it springs from an accurate appraisal of the play-world: the London of *Epicoene* is obsessed with the need to keep up appearances; its concern with a proper decorum hardly touches on the life of the mind, let alone the spirit. Imagination is in short supply there except in organising games of one-upmanship. *The Alchemist* explores a world where imagination is for many the one solace in an otherwise bleak existence: far from inducing stillness and serenity, imagination runs riot and produces nothing but noise and vexation. We pass with lightning speed from a charade of squealing fairies to an erotic encounter between an ageing lecher and a whore in which preposterously he struggles with rhetoric to try and make them 'feel gold, taste gold, hear gold, sleep gold . . . *concumbere* gold' (IV. i. 29–30); then we are plunged into a lesson in speaking with an 'angry tongue', interspersed with a study in incomprehension between a Spaniard and several English-speakers where it is thought that gesture signifies a degree of communication; next Dol in her role of Lord's sister has her 'fit of raving' and screams gibberish which Face and Mammon endeavour to suppress; this is climaxed by a tremendous explosion and a battle royal in which Kastril, Drugger and Ananias shout down Surly. The long-sustained crescendo in sound is beautifully paced and as the decibel count increases, language increasingly parts company with meaning. The presence of syntactical structures only emphasises the outrageous aburdity of what is being uttered:

> Thou art not of the light! That ruff of pride
> About thy neck betrays thee, and is the same
> With that which the unclean birds, in seventy-seven,
> Were seen to prank it with on divers coasts.
>
> (IV. vii. 51–4)

Ananias is denouncing Surly's vast Spanish ruff: oratorical rhythms are being used to give a specious moral weight to what is an expression of bigotry and spite. It is simply rodomontade: so much hot air. Alert as all this makes us in detecting specious assumptions of authority, we cannot but be conscious of the gap between tone and intention in Lovewit as he takes possession of the stage-space in the final scenes. Jonson's strategies in *The Alchemist* increasingly draw our attention to the way people use words as the surest index to their inner natures, to the degree to which their minds and imaginations are disciplined. He works repeatedly by contraries

to have us find directions out: noise educates us in the significance
of tone; from parodies of authority and the aristocratic temper we
are to infer their intrinsic constitution. It is to flatter our powers
of discrimination that Jonson finally shifts Face from the centre of
the stage and gives it over to the even more subtly devious Lovewit.
As Face himself admits in his epilogue there is 'decorum' in this:
it shows a proper humility in a good actor that he can respect the
superior artistry of another. It is a shared epilogue and it is as
performers in a play which, if successful, will be regularly revived
that Lovewit and Face address us, reminding us that every man in
imagination is his own actor, a view of life which clearly has its
thrills and its dangers.

The Alchemist has been the most regularly revived of Jonson's
comedies in the modern theatre but the productions have not
always done the play full justice. Too often it has been presented
as simply a farce with little attention being paid to Jonson's richness
of characterisation. It is the one play of his which directors have
consistently felt free to transpose to more recent times. Griff Rhys
Jones at the Lyric Hammersmith (1985) set the action in Victorian
London, wittily examining through the text the nineteenth-century
ethos of the self-made man. This approach had some cogency, as
did Tyrone Guthrie's up-to-the-minute 1962 version at the Old
Vic which reflected the soul-destroying shabbiness of the ration-
conscious, post-war years in England and the nostalgia for a
lost, largely mythical world of genteel ease. The problem with
productions of this kind, however thoroughly carried out, is that
they tend to emphasise the games with illusion in the play at the
expense of the more astringent qualities in Jonson's writing. All
references to the plague obviously have to be cut whereas in the
original production that constant reminder of Last Things would
have given a particularly pressing anxiety to the gulls' efforts at
self-transcendence: their escapism, as Jonson defines it, is not just
the product of a compulsive taste for fantasising; there are grim
realities hedging round the characters' existence. The distinct
political connotations of the dream-selves tend to be lost sight of
in modern-dress productions too – another aspect of the subtle
differentiations in psychology through which Jonson distinguishes
the various tricksters and gulls in the play. In consequence the
playing tends to be broad, even pedestrian, when nuance and
precision of detail in characterisation are wanted. There is no

denying the play works best when a cast allow the text to evoke a convincing sense of Jacobean London for their audiences. This was certainly the case with Trevor Nunn's production for the Royal Shakespeare Company in 1977 with Ian McKellan and John Woodvine as Face and Subtle. There was a heart-stopping precariousness about it all, which manifested itself in an increasing panic on the part of the gulls as if – deep down – they sensed they were to be baulked of their goals, and in a delirious excitability in the tricksters (Face especially) at what they were nerving themselves to do, as if they were awed by their own audacity. It was exhilarating because it was all *felt* to be dangerous, the anarchy had a plausible manic drive to it, because every development in the action was carefully rooted by Nunn and his cast in character. There is an element of self-consciousness about Ian McKellan's style of acting; it seems intrinsic to the dynamism of his stage-personality as it is to Olivier's or Gielgud's. The energy of his creative intelligence during a performance compels attention, never more so than when a role allows him scope for an exuberance and fervour in his temperament. Nunn wisely built his production around this quality in his Face and made *The Alchemist* less a play about folly or greed than about acting and its ubiquity in human relations. That was to touch the pulse of Jonson's comedy.

7
'Bartholomew Fair'

In *The Alchemist* the device of the play-within-the-play almost threatened to take over the whole structure. Much of the action is taken up with a group of actors devising scenarios for the benefit of one or sometimes two privileged individuals who constitute an audience of a rather special kind. Their patronage buys a private performance which, since the play is designed to realise their most intimate fantasies, begins quickly to engross them in the action. These playlets-within-the-play again and again are transformed into participatory theatre of a highly dubious kind. The device has a long history in Renaissance drama but it had not previously been deployed with such panache as by Jonson here, where it is made into the organising structural principle of his comedy. Customarily the device was used to highlight some celebratory occasion within the world of the play (though dramatists increasingly saw it as a means of subtly heightening and intensifying the themes explored in the play overall). The on-stage audience was generally aristocratic or royal which made the play-within-the-play in some degree an act of homage. This whole pattern of action had its parallel, of course, in historical reality: plays were presented regularly at the English court and many of those chosen for such performances contained eulogy of the reigning monarch implicitly as in *The Merry Wives of Windsor*, or explicitly as in *Cynthia's Revels*. Jonson in *Cynthia's Revels* had envisaged a new kind of court entertainment as one that would pay due homage by exploring as its theme the very nature of courtliness. Queen Elizabeth did not respond to Jonson's prompting in the play that such a style of drama be established as a regular activity at Whitehall; King James, however, did: from 1605 Jonson began devising and steadily perfecting the form of the court masque.

The masque is to be the subject of a later chapter; suffice it here to state that the important element of homage was achieved through the steady transformation of the piece from presentational into participatory theatre. Select members of the royal family and the aristocracy famed for their beauty and grace were decked out magnificently as allegorical representations of the virtues, principles and powers of monarchy and the scenario was wittily devised to explain their emblematic status and their relation to the courtly audience assembled to view the display. The whole scheme was devised to hold a mirror up to the princely nature, temper and sensibility. At a given moment these idealised beings stepped out of the framework of the scenario to choose dancing partners from amongst the audience; masque gave place to court ball as the worlds of stage and auditorium mingled and conjoined. Participating in the masque brought the court (at least in theory if not wholly in practice) to a point of self-transcendence. By the time Jonson wrote *The Alchemist*, he and Inigo Jones after some years' experience had developed the masque to a height of sophistication.

'If I were King for a day' is a near-proverbial form in which people express their dissatisfaction with the ordering of the society in which they live. What Face, Subtle and Dol devise – at a price – are masques for the common man: forms of participatory theatre in which workaday minds fleetingly embrace their most cherished fantasies of themselves as famous, moneyed, powerful. These masques reach for transcendence but have an alarming tendency to disintegrate, leaving each patron-participant acutely aware of the deprivations of his actual daily existence. The self is confirmed, not translated. As so often with Jonson's comedies this all reflects back on his audiences, challenging them to explore the quality of their personal experience in the theatre: is it escapist, merely aesthetic, superior, or educative in the Aristotelian sense? Has the self been confirmed, purged, uplifted, disabused? With marvellous ingenuity Jonson exploits the device of the play-within-the-play in *The Alchemist* both to entertain and to provoke an intense self-consciousness in an audience about their need for and response to the art of performance.

Throughout *Bartholomew Fair*[1] Jonson continued subtly exper-
imenting with the device, but he also chose to include one more
obviously traditional usage of the play-within-the-play: it comes
towards the end of the action, is proffered as an entertainment for
most of the characters we have seen elsewhere and in some measure
it heightens our appreciation of the themes of the play overall. But
there is one major discrepancy from conventional uses of the device:
the performers are all puppets. This is wholly in keeping with the
demotic setting of the play at a popular fair; so too is the style of
play on offer – a bawdy, farcical debunking of a fashionable work
of high culture (Marlowe's *Hero and Leander*) which is transposed
to a Thames-side tavern where it becomes an excuse for much sturdy
knockabout. Clearly more is going on here than a desire on Jonson's
part for authentic realism. There has been some debate about the
kind of puppet Jonson might have had in mind: glove, rod or
marionette. But *kind* is immaterial: whichever sort is used, the
crucial factor is the diminutive size and the manipulated condition
of these performers as compared with their on-stage audience. At
best they could not be more than two feet high: considerably smaller,
therefore, than any boy-actor present. The play-scene in *Hamlet*
poses a director a real problem in performance because of its divided
focus: both 'The Play of Gonzago' and the response of the court-
audience at Elsinore demand our attention; the layout of the scene
on stage has to be carefully thought through if the required balance
of interest is to be met. In the play scene from *Bartholomew Fair*
there are at least fourteen characters on-stage as spectators in the
booth or as manipulators. They are wholly united as audience in the
concentration they give to the puppets, but we know they have got
themselves into some highly divisive predicaments in the course of
a day at the fair and, sensing that the end of the comedy is near, we
expect a catastrophic disruption of the proceedings at any moment.
The small stature of the puppet-performers (compensated for by
their extravagantly vigorous activity) allows us to watch both the
play-within-the-play and the groups of on-stage spectators with ease
and with rapt attention. Once again we have been placed by Jonson
in a position where we can watch and judge the effect of performance:
as an audience we are required to study an audience.

It is a strange creation that Littlewit takes such pride in as
playwright – proof, if by this stage one were needed, of his want
of intellect. Written in jingling doggerel with tiresome repetitions,

and predictable verbal routines, the play of Hero and Leander is nonsense as literary art and as an expression of wit. But it communicates powerfully by non-linguistic means: gesture, sound-patterns, slapstick violence and sheer energy. It is a celebration of mindless, untutored instinct: all the characters are swayed by an appetite for lechery, drink and aggression; the spirit of carnival has run rampant. Yet, instead of finding freedom and release, the characters (by virtue of the conditions of puppet-performance) are seen to be ever more *mechanical* in their drive the more frenetic they become. That the show should be the conception of a respectable proctor in the Archdeacon's Court is bizarre enough but, as the performance continues, Bartholomew Cokes, an 'esquire of Harrow', keeps up a running commentary with all the relish of a connoisseur on its artistry, enquiring into the significance of certain effects, savouring odd turns of phrase, delighting in the moments of spectacle which usually involve a *tour-de-force* in manipulation as when the puppets seem to do battle with their presenter. The absurd incongruity of it all is hilarious. How do Jonson's other spectators react? The folio text of the comedy printed with *The Devil Is An Ass* and *The Staple of News* by John Beale in 1631 is a fascinating document in that it contains numerous directions by Jonson himself about the timing and nature of particular effects and how certain pieces of stage business should be conducted. Interestingly, however, he gave his actors total freedom here in improvising as audience their response to the puppets. Are they silent because they are engrossed in imagination by the play, or are they uproariously voluble, taking the lead from Cokes's expressions of delight and approval? Or are they perhaps stunned into silence by the accuracy of the play's depiction of licence and its relevance to them? Are their responses individual or corporate? Several of the persons present have indulged a longing for pork or ale and are now being tempted to gratify their sexual urges. Others have suffered repeated drubbings from total strangers. Hero is about to give herself in the play to a man she but chanced to encounter, whose naked legs have excited her into making 'a sheep's eye and a half' at him; watching her is Grace Wellborn, the Ward, who has just promised her hand in marriage to Winwife after two hours' acquaintance, when all she knows of him is that he has a courteous and apparently caring manner. The intricacies in the plot of the puppet play are to be unravelled by the arrival of King Dionysus translated, to fit the decorum of low comedy, into a scrivener (even as Cupid has been turned into the tavern barman); similarly the local magistrate, Justice Overdo, habited in the disguise of a porter, is waiting for the ideal moment to reveal himself and expose the iniquity of all present. Whether actors choose to play the on-stage spectators as aware of the parallels between the puppets and themselves or not is immaterial: either way they stand under correction, even as the puritan Zeal-of-the-Land Busy is soon to be put firmly in his place by a puppet when he tries to disrupt the show on the grounds that it is profane and obscene.

The terms of Busy's attack are worth pondering on:

> I will remove Dagon there, I say, that idol, that heathenish idol, that remains, as I may say, a beam, a very beam, not a beam of the sun, nor a beam of the moon, nor a beam of a balance, neither a house-beam, nor a weaver's beam, but a beam in the eye, in the eye of the Brethren; a very great beam, an exceeding great beam; such as are your stage-players, rhymers, and morris-dancers, who have walked hand in hand, in contempt of the Brethren, and the Cause; and been borne out by instruments of no mean countenance.   (V. v. 4–12)

The allusion to St Matthew's gospel (vii. 3–5) and the figure of the mote and the beam is clear; so too is Busy's total misunderstanding of Christ's words which insist on tact and scruple in judging lest the critic be found guilty of a worse sin than the man who stands under his accusation. The figure is exemplifying one of Christ's principal *dicta*: 'Judge not, lest ye be judged'. This is a disconcerting allusion coming precisely where it does in the play – at the very moment when we might feel tempted to consider ourselves superior to all the characters on-stage and dismiss them as knaves and fools. We know by this time that Busy himself is not only a great hypocrite but also a crook, 'making himself rich by being made feoffee in trust to deceased Brethren and cozening their heirs by swearing the absolute gift of their inheritance (V. ii. 64–6). Repeatedly throughout *Bartholomew Fair* Jonson devises tactics, alienation effects, to make his audience conscious of their complex and creative relation to the play in performance. The puppet play is in fact the best and most intricate of a carefully

graduated sequence of strategies, which simultaneously entertain
while inviting us to explore our laughter and so probe deeply into
the psychology of performance and audience-response.

Surprisingly, *Bartholomew Fair* has often been considered shape-
less. Dr John Brown in 1765, invited to revise the comedy for a
possible production by Garrick, opined that 'the comedy was, in
its essentials, *excellent*', then added that '*it wanted nothing but a
plan*'.[2] Brown's view was presumably persuasive since Garrick
never attempted a revival, though he had a success with the more
rambling structure of *Every Man In His Humour*; it could not
have been the *low* comedy of *Bartholomew Fair* that frightened
him off, since his own role of Abel Drugger in *The Alchemist* was
frequently singled out in theatre criticism of the period as the acme
of achievement in the low comic style. The play has had a
respectable number of revivals this century but they have sometimes given audiences the impression of being meandering, lacking
in dramatic climaxes or thematic cohesion.[3] After the immensely
taut structure of *The Alchemist*, *Bartholomew Fair* might appear
loosely constructed, but it is only an appearance. Jonson does
pose director and cast a teaser in that the comedy in performance
should create the illusion of random chance occurrence on the
surface while making an audience sense – beyond the attempt at
stage realism in presenting life at a fair – the discipline of rigorous
intellectual structure. *Bartholomew Fair* is at once the most
prodigally expansive of Jonson's plays with its cast of thirty-three
speaking roles and his most carefully crafted (the 1631 text divides
the comedy into five acts each with six scenes). Numerous strands
of plot are developed together and interwoven coherently and
deftly; at one moment one has a sense of the plausible passing of
time, at others one is made to feel that episodes played concurrently
are in fact happening simultaneously in different or adjacent parts
of the fair. We never lose sight of any particular group of characters
for long enough to allow the tension or interest in their predicament
to flag. It helps that the fairground setting allows Jonson to keep
one group of characters (the visitors) continually on the move
while the rest (the stallholders) are necessarily static so we have a
sense of continual circling about a series of notable fixed points –
Ursula's booth, the stocks, Lantern's puppet show – which allow
us to keep our bearings in the general *mêlée*. It is the nature and
the associations of those three centres of action – for the satisfaction

of appetites and exercise of bodily functions; for correction; for
entertainment and imaginative release – that help to focus our
attention on the inner thematic dimensions of the comedy and its
preoccupation with judgement on human nature.

The play begins with one of Jonson's funniest and most inventive
Inductions that wittily intimates all the themes that are to be
explored later in depth. The stagekeeper appears on the sly, taking
advantage of consternation backstage when it is found that the
stockings of the first character to appear need a quick darn. He
warns us not to expect much of the play since it lacks in his view
all the best features of a *real* fairground – the eccentrics; the
trained animals; the smutty sideshows; the horseplay; the time-
honoured, familiar patter and routines of the clowns and zanies.
With a quick glance over his shoulder to see if Jonson or his
assistant have caught sight of him, he goes on to give the thumbs
down to 'master poets' who won't do their proper research but
will trust to their own dull invention. He is interrupted in mid-
peroration by the prompter and a scrivener who ridicule his
presumption to stand as critic when, as stage-sweeper, he is fit
only to hobnob with the groundlings. The prompter then officiously
instructs the scrivener to read an indenture that sets out certain
'articles of agreement' between Jonson and the audience in which
the dramatist guarantees us our money's worth of enjoyment
providing we fulfil certain conditions in our turn: that throughout
we will be completely at ease with ourselves; that we will be quite
open to the experience offered us and not churlishly hope for a
play written either to worn-out or to currently modish conventions;
that we should accept that any play will establish its own particular
decorum and related criteria defining verisimilitude, so we should
not be disappointed if we fail to get romantic transformations after
the fashion recently set by Shakespeare; and, if we should sense a
satirical impulse at work in the comedy, we should not suppose it
directed at specific individuals. With remarkable economy of stage-
time Jonson has set our minds thinking about questions of dramatic
realism and decorum of style and their relation to modes of
perception and judgement. He warns us that we are not going to
be allowed to rest apathetically content with a play written to
popular formulae: we have our contribution to bring to the
performance, which he trusts will be a generous engagement, not
a critical superiority. He presents this material through three

contrasting voices: one earthy, one primly condescending and one flatly impersonal and legal. This perfectly demonstrates Jonson's theme – that judgement is subjective, impressionistic, and immediately reflects on the character of the speaker.

Hanging uneasily over the Induction, giving an edge to the laughter, is the awareness that judgement can lead to censure or correction. What if the articles of agreement are broken? Legal contracts usually contain penalty clauses. How are we to stand reproved in this instance? We are offered one developed and graphic image of correction when the Stagekeeper regrets there will be no pump on stage which, he argues, could have been the settting for a rare bit of farce: 'a punk set under upon her head with her stern upward, and ha' been soused by my witty young masters o' the Inns o' Court' (Induction, ll. 29–31). When he suggested this to the playwright, Jonson's response, he tells us, was to call him an ass. The implication of the Stagekeeper's tone is that this would be genial and permissible horseplay on the grounds that lads will be lads and whores are fair game given their antisocial activities. The judgement implicit in the observation is stereotyped, sexist and callous. It is noticeable that though the threat of correction is always present in the play (Justice Overdo vows to castigate richly all enormities he detects at the fair), it never actually materialises. Ironically three figures of Authority who continually talk of punishment for wrongdoing and are highly suspicious of the fairground folk are the only ones who suffer physically as the butt of horseplay or find themselves exposed to humiliation in the stocks. This considerably affects their perception and tempers their judgement. Noticeably the recent productions which reviewers have found confusing tend to be ones where the director has omitted the Induction. Given a play of the length of *Bartholomew Fair* that is an understandable but fatal decision, since as a prologue it subtly establishes the linguistic and thematic parameters within which the ensuing comedy will work. Most importantly the Induction alerts an audience's wits to their relation to the play being performed: the articles of agreement define our role as seriously active not passive. *Bartholomew Fair* is to be an exercising of our moral imaginations.

After whetting our appetite for the sights of the fair, Jonson then proceeds to delay taking us there for a whole act. Instead we are asked first to watch all but one (Overdo) of the chief visitors to the fairground in a setting which defines their status and activities as citizens. A different kind of exposition would have allowed Jonson to convey most of the basic facts about these characters as they arrived in their several groups at Smithfield, had he so wished. Clearly he had an objective in showing these individuals at home, paying neighbourly visits, doing business together. After Jonson's injunction about not expecting a dated or fashionable type of comedy we might be forgiven for expressing some surprise at the people he introduces to us, as they are the recognisable types we associate with City Comedy, and especially Middleton's version of the genre: a law-man and his wife; two puritans; two men about town, both somewhat down-at-heel and consequently on the make, one with more than a hint of a taste for roaring; a country clodpoll (who is also heir to a good estate) accompanied by his tutor, a bride-to-be (a ward of court) and his sister (a magistrate's spouse). Much potential for comedy might grow simply out of their social relations together, but that is not to be Jonson's aim: the comedy is to reside in how they individually respond when their social groups get dispersed, fragmented and then realigned at the fair. Jonson quickly establishes that a fair, in the eyes of people who wish to be thought respectable, is not a place where one should risk being seen, since it is a demotic resort. Cokes, the simpleton, wishes to go for innocent enjoyment, however, and, though they resent it, his party is powerless to prevent him dragging them along in his wake. Quarlous and Winwife, the two gallants, promptly abandon their plans for the day and go in pursuit of Cokes ostensibly for the 'excellent creeping sport' of watching a fool and his money being parted, though they seem also to be strangely taken with his betrothed, the ward.

The proctor has the most pressing reason to go to Smithfield since he fancies himself as a wit and has composed the puppet play to be performed there. He and his wife have to find a reason for going that will be acceptable to her mother, Mistress Purecraft, and her mentor, Zeal-of-the-Land Busy, who are elect puritans. They hit on the idea that Win, who is in the early weeks of pregnancy, should pretend to an overwhelming longing in the fashion traditionally expected of one in her condition to eat pork in a fairbooth. The ruse works: Purecraft can deny her child nothing and she has little trouble persuading Busy to justify their going on the expedition on religious grounds since he has a prodigious appetite for food himself and a wonderful facility for manipulating language to extol anything he might choose to do as proof of his elect state:

> . . . it may be eaten, and in the Fair, I take it, in a booth, the tents of the wicked. The place is not much, not very much; we may be religious in midst of the profane, so it be eaten with a reformed mouth, with sobriety, and humbleness; not gorged in with gluttony or greediness: there's the fear; for, should she go there, as taking pride in the place, or delight in the unclean dressing, to feed the vanity of the eye or the lust of the palate, it were not well, it were not fit, it were abominable, and not good.   (I. vi. 70–8)

Anything, then, in Busy's view, is to be permitted, provided the attitude of mind in which one undertakes it is felt by one's self to be correct. Win's attitude is total glee at the success of her deception, particularly since she is aware she is merely following her mother's example, making a great noise to get her will. The dialogue that leads up to Win's demonstration of desperate yearning deserves close scrutiny:

> LITTLEWIT: Cut thy lace i' the mean time and play the hypocrite, sweet Win.
> WIN: No, I'll not make me unready for it. I can be hypocrite enough, though I were never so strait-laced.
> LITTLEWIT: You say true. You have been bred i' the family, and brought up to't. Our mother is a most elect hypocrite, and has maintained us all this seven year with it, like gentlefolks.
> WIN: Ay, let her alone, John; she is not a wise wilful widow for nothing, nor a sanctified sister for a song. And let me alone too; I ha' somewhat o' the mother in me; you shall see.   (I. v. 149–59)

The movement of the passage towards the final pun ('I ha' somewhat o' the mother in me') brilliantly demonstrates how ingrained a habit of her disposition is Win's duplicity: she will take advantage of being with child to feign a 'mother' (in the sense of hysteria), conscious that in so doing she is merely proving herself her mother's daughter, being wisely wilful in the interest of personal gain; and she takes pride in her inheritance: she has been bred to be shameless. The ingenuity of her manipulation of people's perception of her finds its exact correlative in the ingenuity with which Win manipulates language to express her innermost self and both are a source of delight to her, quite unlike the heavy earnestness of Busy's linguistic mannerisms or the self-conscious effortfulness of Littlewit's.

Win's other pun in this exchange about being a hypocrite though 'never so strait-laced' (playing as it does on the contradictory ideas of fashionable corseting to offset the figure and of an austerely strict morality) again nicely captures the comic inconsistencies in her character, but in a way that leads us closer to sensing the function this first act seems designed to serve. The fair is soon to work some remarkable transformations in these citizens, many of which will have long-term repercussions. But what Act One establishes is that these changes are not total reversals of character, rather the licence obtaining at the fair releases qualities which are already present in the citizens' various temperaments but which have not yet found forceful expression. One advantage of using recognisable stereotypes of city comedy here is that the characters' *respectable* identities, the projected selves they sustain in Act One, remain firmly in our minds while they are undergoing change. Respectability and class-superiority are found to be the thinnest of veneers; a more urgent, wayward self lurks perilously close to the surface in all of them, except Cokes, who has retained a childhood innocence into manhood and is thus blissfully himself at the fair, quickly resilient to all the adversities that afflict him and quite unperturbed by the transformations the others are undergoing. Veneers in furniture-making generally embellish the commonest woods which are used as an understructure because of their inherent strengths. The citizens are consistently disabused of their pretensions at the fair and forced to recognise their common humanity; but Jonson is too subtle a dramatist to make this process of change simply a sequence in which one by one numerous egos are systematically deflated. Much of the fun of the play comes from our sense of how fitting the declensions are in each case, given the insight that we formed into the characters during the opening act.

Long before we hear about the practised hypocrisy of Purecraft's household, we are amused at the incongruity between Win's sober-seeming environment and her fashionable appearance with 'her fine high shoes like the Spanish lady' and her knock-out line in hats that has her husband in ecstasies. Love of finery will prove her undoing in time. Then we note how easy-going her husband is about sharing her favours among his friends: the moment Winwife and Quarlous appear they are invited to kiss her ('I envy no man my delicates'). Winwife – characteristically as we are to discover – steals a single peck and romantically apostrophises Win's 'strawberry breath, cherry-lips, apricot-cheeks'; Quarlous, always more forward, does not scruple to take advantage of the offer and rain kisses on her till Win grows uneasy and Winwife requests him to 'forbear, for my respect somewhat'. Littlewit finds in the situation matter only for a laboured pun on his own name and is oblivious of the tension that Quarlous has provoked and is clearly enjoying. Kissing is relatively rare in Renaissance drama and an episode involving a woman being 'kissed in general' like this has few counterparts. The most notable case outside Jonson's own later work is Shakespeare's scene showing Cressida's arrival in the Greek camp where she is laughingly kissed by most of the Argive leaders in turn, which causes Ulysses to think her a 'daughter of the game'.[4] When in the puppet-play Hero is found embracing Leander in public, Pythias observes 'What's here? What's here? Kiss, kiss upon kiss' and Damon concludes 'Mistress Hero's a whore' (V. iv. 292–4).

At the fair a near-identical pattern of events takes place. His hunger satisfied, Littlewit is anxious to know if preparations for the puppet show are going well and at the first opportunity leaves Win in the care of two chance acquaintances, Knockem and Whit, whom he believes are 'honest gentleman' simply on the grounds that they kindly persuaded Ursula, who runs the pig-booth, to lend Win a receptacle in which to relieve herself. 'Good company' they may be, but Knockem and Whit are bawds likely soon to be 'undone for want of fowl i' the Fair'. Ursula advises they force Win 'to become a bird o' the game' (IV. v. 15–18). We have several times seen how accurately Knockem can read people's innermost characters from their appearance – a necessary skill if he is to frame his approach to possible clients judiciously. He now commiserates with Win on the 'dull' life that an honest woman has in comparison with that of a real lady; seeking an instance of the greater freedom she might have, he turns instantly to matters of dress; pointing out how a lady has 'her wires, and her tires, her green gowns, and velvet petticoats' (IV. v. 35–6). Knockem can read, as we have learned to do, the full significance of Win's clothes; Win herself has led too sheltered a life to understand the implications of the finery they are offering her. Having set her pulse racing with thoughts of dress and status, Whit and Knockem proceed to enumerate other pleasures of precisely the kind that has enticed her and her husband to the fair for the day: theatres, supping with gallants, tippling. To Win indulgence offers a form of freedom, as the opening act made clear; her one scruple now is whether she can keep up an appearance of honesty. Knockem plays his trump-card in reply, appealing to her desire to be always modish: 'It is the vapour of spirit in the wife to cuckold, nowadays, as it is the vapour of fashion in the husband not to suspect' (IV. v. 48–50). Even when Ramping Alice in all the insignia of the professional bursts on to the stage to complain how lately 'poor common whores can ha' no traffic for the privy rich ones' (IV. v. 68–9), Win makes no connection between the punk and the image planted in her mind by Knockem. Transformed on her next appearance into a 'green' woman, she relaxes in the arms of a man we know to be a cutpurse, but in imagination she is clearly living a charmed life as a great lady with an attentive admirer ('they do so all-to-be-madam me' V. iv. 41–2). Hilarious as Win's transformation is, there is an exact psychological logic controlling its development out of the comic incongruities we noted on her first appearance. We noted them and laughed; Knockem noted them, surmised their implication and put them to his use.

Some of the transformations are more abrupt. Busy is all noise in his zealous denunciation of the ungodliness of the world he sees about him. Nothing except his rapacious eating stops the thunder of his rhetoric, not even being put in the stocks for causing a breach of the peace; that to him is merely proof that the elect are chosen for their power to withstand insult and suffering. There is no profundity in what he utters, merely oratorical insistence that his perception of things is the true one: confronted by Pocher, the beadle, threatening imprisonment, Busy rejoices that such a 'minister of darkness . . . canst not rule my tongue', since 'my tongue it is mine own' (IV. i. 87–8). The only possible transformation Busy could undergo is into silence and it is left to a puppet finally to effect that change by patiently but relentlessly contradicting Busy's every assertion till he asks for proof. Puppet shows puritan that they are actually alike in that each speaks 'by inspiration'. He then argues that puppets are incapable of committing the offence levelled by the puritan at actors (that, in contradiction of the law set out in Deuteronomy, they dress in the clothes of the opposite sex) since puppets are sexless and he 'takes up his garment' in Busy's face as proof. Describing the puritan's zeal as 'malicious, purblind', he pushes his triumph home by drawing yet more analogies between the two of them: 'my standing is as lawful as his . . . I have as little to do with learning as he; and do scorn her helps as much as he' (V. v. 103–5). Busy stands condemned as bogus, vicious, ignorant and, by subtle implication, impotent; his mode of judgement has been turned wittily against himself. He suffers 'conversion' to a passive spectator in the puppet-booth and remains silent for the duration of Jonson's comedy.

Busy's fate has been anticipated in part by what happens to the tutor, Wasp. He is a tetchy individual, constantly finding cause to disagree with everyone present to the extent that it is hardly surprising his pupil, Cokes, is a nincompoop since he can never have been given any firm directions about behaviour. Wasp assumes a voice of authority but, as with Busy, it is an empty mannerism. His tone is continually patronising, which suggests a weary desperation with the stupidity and irrationality of human-kind. The manifest reason for his failure as a teacher is that he has absolutely no respect for his charge: he assumes all the time that Cokes will make a fool of himself, so inevitably he does. Jonson gets a lot of comic mileage at Wasp's expense out of this psychological insight. The moment the fair is mentioned Cokes is avid to go for all Wasp's efforts to dissuade him – learn from past experience he will not:

> If he go to the Fair, he will buy of everything to a baby there; and household stuff for that too. If a leg or an arm on him did not grow on, he would lose it i' the press. Pray heaven I bring him off with one stone! And then he is such a ravener after fruit! You will not believe what a coil I had t'other day to compound a business between a Catherine-pear-woman and him about snatching! (I. v. 107–13)

This is almost exactly the scenario of what will happen at Smithfield – Cokes loses two purses, his marriage licence and his betrothed in no time and snatching again after pears costs him his hat, cloak and sword. While he still has his money about him, he cannot make up his mind what to purchase since all the goods on display at Leatherhead's stall are so tempting; Wasp, when he overhears the list of things Cokes plans to acquire, tartly adds: 'No, the shop; buy the whole shop, it will be best; the shop, the shop!' (III. iv. 75–6). Sarcasm is lost on Cokes: he promptly buys up all Leatherhead's wares and the neighbouring gingerbread stall too. Wasp repeatedly plants the idea for Cokes's next silliness in his head, then is appalled to watch his worst fears being realised: experience teaches nothing to master or charge.

Jonson allows Wasp two scenes in which we see him relaxed and free briefly from his responsibility as tutor. Deep in his cups with a circle of fairground folk, he joins in their game of vapours which requires 'every man to oppose the last man that spoke'. This clearly touches a responsive chord in Wasp's peevish disposition and he plays with joyful abandon while drunkenly asserting: 'I have no reason, nor will I hear of no reason, nor will I look for no reason, and he is an ass that either knows any or looks for't from me' (IV. iv. 40–2) and 'I am not i' the right, nor never was i' the right, nor never will be i' the right, while I am in my right mind' (IV. iv. 67–9). Play has brought a sad truth to light and the judgement is on his own lips. Later when he is arrested by the watch for unruly behaviour and placed in the stocks, Wasp cunningly escapes by playing a schoolboy's trick: he puts his shoe on his hand and thrusts his arm in the hole where his feet should go; getting away is simple once the watch are not looking. All that his years of schoolmastering have taught him is how to elude detention; noticeably he can command no authority either of voice or presence to avoid arrest. Apprised accidentally of Wasp's being stocked for misconduct, Cokes cannot resist playfully teasing him on the subject when they meet up again at the puppet booth; Wasp is overcome with remorse and self-pity: 'I must think no longer to reign, my government is at an end. He that will correct another must want fault in himself' (V. iv. 97–8). Cokes's ensuing aside is significant: 'Sententious Numps! I never heard so much from him before'. Wasp's exhortations have been no more but noise till this moment, to which Cokes has never troubled to listen; Numps's powers of suasion have all been at a subliminal level. Now that his tutor is humbled and suffering, Cokes is inclined to be attentive; but Wasp bids him concentrate on the puppets and lapses into mortified silence: he cannot rise to a laugh at his own expense which might create a whole new style of relationship between them. Cokes is clearly hurt by Wasp's manner but tries again to be gracious and caring ('Do not think on't, I have forgot it. 'Tis but a nine days' wonder, man; let it not trouble thee'); he gets snapped at for his pains: 'I would the stocks were about your neck, sir' (V. iv. 191–3). Wasp's mortification is judgement upon him. Despite the epic dimensions of the play Jonson continually finds time for subtly revealing insights into his characters; and the director must make time for them to carry effect too. Jonson may introduce the citizens to us as stereotypes but he endows them steadily with an unexpected complexity.[5]

This is particularly true of the third member of the motley crew who find themselves in the stocks together: thrust in with Busy and Wasp is Adam Overdo for whom the experience is highly embarrassing since he, a Justice of the Peace, has been arrested (wrongfully) for theft. We did not see Overdo amongst the citizens in Act One who were gathering together and finding occasions for taking themselves off to the Fair; he was already at Smithfield not in pursuit of thrills and enjoyment but out of a pressing sense of the responsibilities of his office. Convinced that the times are iniquitous and that the fair is a centre of crime and of sly practices to defraud honest, decent citizens, Overdo has donned a disguise as a mendicant preacher, Mad Arthur of Bradley, the better to penetrate the circles of the fairfolk to scent out enormities. And so he lurks suspiciously round the periphery of the action, becoming himself an object of suspicion on account of his weird behaviour when crimes are actually committed. The ruler or magistrate who goes out into the world in disguise to learn the ways of the people had an honourable heritage in Renaissance drama; Shakespeare and Marston amongst Jonson's immediate contemporaries had explored the situation on more than one occasion; by 1614 the device was getting to be somewhat hackneyed. Jonson gives us more than a hint that Overdo's imagination in the matter has been somewhat coloured by theatrical precedent. The justice yearns to be like the Duke in *Measure for Measure* or Prospero and stage a grand *coup de théâtre* with the revelation of his true identity as the climax: were his scheme to go according to plan (and he has the rhetoric of denunciation for a set-piece of oratory all prepared), he could then place everyone in a careful order before him and, like an all-seeing Olympian, unravel the intricate network of their relations in a spectacular denouement. Overdo forgets that Prospero had magic arts to assist him in the ordering of his island and, more crucially, that Vincentio in *Measure for Measure* was frequently discomfited on account of his disguise while trying to bring a semblance of moral order to his Vienna.

Amusingly the fair shows up Overdo as a complete innocent. He may have on his lips Cicero's words of disgust at Cataline's evil in Rome but reading the classics (like seeing contemporary plays) has done little to tutor Overdo's imagination except to excite in him a taste for grandiloquence: he misunderstands most of what he overhears and invariably fails to see what precisely is happening around him. (Overdo is a wonderful device in moments of complex plotting for keeping the audience on the *qui vive*.) He twice mistakes genial banter amongst the stallholders about the shoddiness of the goods they severally have on offer for the truth, yet fails to respond in any way whatever when Quarlous, one of the gallants, starts a railing match with Ursula, the pig-woman, and pushes it to the point where he deliberately provokes a fray that more than disturbs the peace. He becomes solicitous for the future well-being of a decent-looking young man he sees frequenting the company at Ursula's booth because he has the suggestion about him of being a good clerk in the making. Set on the right tracks, Overdo supposes, he would prove 'a quick hand'. When one of the fair folk laughingly acquiesces – 'A very quick hand, sir' – he never supposes this is a reference to Edgeworth's proven skill as a cutpurse (II. iv. 33–4). Edgeworth twice steals a purse in front of Overdo's eyes and both times contrives to get Overdo himself accused of the theft, yet Overdo continues to believe Edgeworth (not himself) is the innocent soul lost in a benighted world and in need of friendly guidance. Meanwhile his wife and his ward, who should be the objects of his care, are going fearfully astray. Mistress Overdo for all her fine clothes and pretensions to matronly dignity renders herself insensible with drink and gets taken up by Knockem and Whit who offer her out as a prostitute. Grace, bitterly resenting Overdo's power (which he bought from the Court of Wards) to shape her future by marrying her to his brother-in-law, the asinine Cokes, circumspectly attaches herself to two likely young men when she gets separated from the rest of her party and adroitly arranges matters so that both agree to respect her honour in return for the promise that she will wed one of them. Which will receive her hand in marriage is a matter she will leave for time and chance to determine. Though a victim of cruel chance as a Ward of Court, she now decides, reckless in desperation, to let 'Destiny [have] a high hand in business of this nature' (IV. iii. 47–8). Her behaviour seems the more absurd given our awareness that her predicament in Overdo's household has brought her a considerable shrewdness of insight and self-knowledge:

> Subtlety would say to me, I know, he [Cokes] is a fool, and has an estate, and I might govern him, and enjoy a friend beside. But these are not my aims. I must have a husband I must love, or I cannot live with him. I shall ill make one of these politic wives.   (IV. iii. 12–15)

Fate will play her a cruel card and as a direct consequence of Overdo's well-intentioned stupidity.

It is here that we can perceive another instance of the rich patterning within Jonson's comedy. The large cast of characters allows him to create a network of parallels and contrasts through which he can illuminate and develop his theme about the precarious nature of judgement when it is based on relativities not absolutes. Stupidity in Busy is compounded with bigotry, in Wasp with a dogmatic insistence and an irascible temper; in Overdo it is coupled with an utter naïvety about the ways of the world. This is both funny because of his position as justice and unsettling because, unlike his companions in the stocks, he is generously disposed towards his fellow men and he does have a strong sense of the demands of his office – at least in theory. He is rendered silly by his own acute anxiety to be seen to do well in a role for which he is not temperamentally or intellectually suited: his choice of role-models from the stage makes that abundantly clear. Then there is the vexing problem of Trouble-all, one time under-officer to Overdo, whom he sacked during the previous year's fair. Trouble-all has been so impressed by the weight of Overdo's power that he now roams the fairground questioning everyone he meets whether they have due authority for what they are doing and will admit no authority but Overdo's as valid. He is the only person in the play who is in any way affected by Overdo or who shows the magistrate a proper respect; in fact his deference has become so obsessive it has quite unhinged his mind. Trouble-all is a splendid conception; he does not enter the action until Act Four, by which stage the fair has begun fully to work on the citizens and relax their defences. In consequence Trouble-all's intrusive questions about proper warrants for their activities allow us quickly to gauge the degree to which they have each decided to set conscience aside and be shameless. Most people find him merely irritating; Grace puts him to use as the chance stranger who will decide which of her escorts she will wed; Edgeworth, flush from yet another theft, is momentarily startled ('Guilt's a terrible thing!') but instantly turns to planning his next venture; Knockem coolly invites Trouble-all to share a drink and, when the madman refuses unless he can produce Overdo's signature, blithely forges one on a scrap of paper; Dame Purecraft, who thrives as a puritan by manipulating the consciences of others, falls besottedly in love with him. Overdo alone genuinely experiences guilt when faced by Trouble-all's plight and determines to bring him some sort of recompense. Unfortunately his good intentions are set at nought by Quarlous, ever the opportunist, who on seeing Trouble-all, decides to find a false beard to match the madman's, steal his clothes and impersonate him in the hope of getting useful knowledge of people's secrets.

One of the most attractive features of Overdo has been his capacity to enjoy a joke at his own expense. Beaten when in his disguise as Mad Arthur by Wasp who suspects him of stealing Cokes's purse, Overdo bears it all with fortitude in the interests of his 'public good design'; but subsequently he is much amused by a plan to 'make very good mirth with it at supper' when he will tell his family who it was they allowed to be cuffed so vigorously: 'they shall ha' it 'i their dish, i' faith, at night for fruit; I love to be merry at my table' (III. iii. 6, 19–20). Geniality, fortitude, responsibility, conscience and generosity are undeniably valuable qualities in a magistrate but only if they accompany the one attribute Overdo significantly lacks: insight. The only citizen who possesses insight in abundance is Quarlous, but he invariably uses his knowledge to jeer at the shortcomings of others. This tone is established immediately on his entry into the action when he sneers

at his friend Winwife's habit of paying court to widows in the hope
of bettering his fortunes. ('There cannot be an ancient tripe or
trillibub i'the town, but thou art straight nosing it.' I. iii. 61–2)
Any suggestion that this might be just affectionate banter between
mates who know the world is quickly dispelled by Quarlous'
insistent and elaborately detailed expression of disgust at the
thought of having sex with a crone:

> Thou must visit 'em as thou wouldst do a tomb, with a torch,
> or three handfuls of link, flaming hot, and so thou mayst hap to
> make 'em feel thee, and after, come to inherit according to thy
> inches.   (I. iii. 69–72)

Quarlous continually pushes his observations too far, making jokes
out of an evident distaste for the facts of human frailty. He starts
a roaring match with fat Ursula at the fair but soon turns from
witty ripostes to the scabrously abusive. Quarlous and Overdo are
regularly on stage together observing the behaviour of other
people at Smithfield: where the magistrate fails to make necessary
connections or often even see what is really going on, the wide
boy never misses a trick. When Busy sits down dumbstruck at the
puppet show, Overdo decides the great moment of reckoning has
come: he sheds his disguise and begins industriously to arrange
everyone before him in groups like sheep and goats to await his
sentence. Scarcely has he got into his rhetorical stride when
Quarlous appears dressed up as Trouble-all hotly pursued by a
near-naked Trouble-all in quest of his clothes. Quarlous confesses
to his real identity then makes himself master of the situation by
instructing Overdo as to the true moral identity of everyone else
present, thereby exposing Overdo himself as wholly devoid of
intelligence and insight. He finally suggests the justice should
relieve a difficult situation by assuming the role he is best fitted
for, that of genial host, and invite everyone home for supper where
they can 'drown the memory of all enormity in your bigg'st bowl'
(V. vi. 100).

Overdo dons a disguise in order to be a passive spectator of
other people's actions; he intends to use his observations for
purposes of moral enlightenment; his problem as audience of the
scenes played out before him at the fair is that he lacks objectivity
and a proper imaginative engagement, what Keats was to term

'negative capability': Overdo sees only what he wants and expects to see, since his epic purpose weighs so heavily on him that it totally controls his mode of perception, even when he gets caught up in the action and becomes an unwilling participant. He has a completely closed mind. Quarlous assumes a disguise for opportunistic reasons – because he is itching to know whether he or Winwife is to be the husband for Grace selected by Trouble-all. Assuming by his apparel that he is the real Trouble-all, Purecraft and Overdo in turn confess their most intimate selves to him. Purecraft tells of her desires, her hypocrisy, her cunning abuse of the practices of her faith to amass a fortune and offers herself in marriage; Overdo speaks simply of his longing to find a way to salve his conscience over Trouble-all. Purecraft was earlier the occasion for Quarlous' outburst of disgust at Winwife's 'exercise of widow-hunting'; he has no qualms now about accepting her himself, given the financial incentives: 'Why should not I marry this six-thousand pound, now I think on't? . . . It is money that I want. Why should I not marry the money, when 'tis offered me?' (V. ii. 72, 76–7). Overdo decides to give Trouble-all an open warrant to deal with as best suits his needs but unwittingly gives it to the disguised Quarlous. He promptly makes it into a deed of gift of the ward, Grace, who in consequence must 'pay him value' on her estate once she weds Winwife. The Littlewits are not likely to be maintained for the future 'like gentlefolks' once Quarlous has the ordering of Purecraft's household; and though Winwife's courtesy to women has been rewarded with an heiress for wife, his rivalry with Quarlous has resulted in a considerable depletion of her dowry. Quarlous watches the world of the fair with rapt attention; when he sees Edgeworth's dexterity as a thief, he blackmails him into stealing Cokes's marriage licence presumably with a view to entering his own name alongside Grace's until she forestalls that scheme with her game with chance. Quarlous is never at a loss: being without integrity or consistency, he is ever-adaptable, quick to manipulate circumstances to his advantage. Whether as spectator or actor he preserves a studied detachment the better to serve his own interests when the moment is judged ripe for action. His judgement (in every sense of the word) is exact but that still renders him coldly pragmatic and antisocial; no warmth of feeling colours either his language or his relations with others; if he has a creative imagination, it is centred entirely on himself.

Twice at Smithfield Quarlous is approached in friendly fashion

by one of the fair folk: Knockem invites him to tobacco or to a
punk and a pig at Ursula's (II. v. 20–40); later Whit offers to 'help
tee to a vife vorth forty marks' (III. ii. 7). Both get the cold
shoulder for their pains and abuse when they persist in pushing
the acquaintance. When Ezekiel hands over the newly stolen
licence to Quarlous, he too tries to hobnob as with an equal,
proferring a part-share in 'a silken gown, a velvet petticoat, or a
wrought smock' (IV. vi. 19–20). Quarlous is outraged by the
implied intimacy: 'Keep it for your companions in beastliness, I
am none of 'em, sir . . . talk not to me, the hangman is only fit to
discourse with you; the hand of beadle is too merciful a punishment
for your trade of life' (IV. vi. 22–8). This is characteristic of the
citizens in general: they gladly avail themselves of the services of
the fair folk then, when their desires are gratified, turn on them a
tone of supercilious scorn. Busy for one eats hugely at Ursula's
booth then anatomises her by way of thanks as 'having the marks
upon her of the three enemies of man: the World, as being in the
Fair; the Devil, as being in the fire; and the Flesh, as being herself'
(III. vi. 33–5). The fact that the situation is repeated three times
with Quarlous suggests that more is at work here than merely a
characterising of him as hypocritical.

   The fair folk are all shown to be, like Quarlous, shrewd observers
of other people: they have to be; their living depends on that skill.
They have instantly to get the measure of a potential customer to
know how to frame a suitable approach. They are all as adept as
Knockem is with Win in reading character from the tell-tale details
that intimate the human frailties beneath the role of respectable
citizen that the visitors to the fair assume. Long before Jonson
takes us to Lantern's puppet booth and asks us to view not only
the play-within-the-play but also the audience watching it, he has
been presenting us with analogous situations in which one group
of characters choose to behave as spectators of another group,
who all unconsciously in going about their business act for their
edification; and repeatedly we as theatre-audience are invited to
watch not only these playlets within the structure of the main play
(as also happened in *The Alchemist*) but also the responses of the
various audiences to what they see. When for example, the puritans
arrive at Ursula's booth led by Busy huffing like a hound after the
scent of pig, their approach is viewed first by Knockem and Whit
and subsequently by Ursula and Mooncalf. Once Busy and his

tribe have entered the booth, there is a rapid discussion between Ursula and her assistants about what these particular puritans offer them in the way of business:

URSULA: Are these the guests o' the game you promised to fill my pit withal today?

KNOCKEM: Ay, what ail they, Urs?

URSULA: Ail they? They are all sippers, sippers o' the City. They look as they would not drink off two penn'orth of bottle-ale amongst 'em.

MOONCALF: A body may read that i' their small printed ruffs.

KNOCKEM: Away, thou art a fool, Urs, and thy Mooncalf too, i' your ignorant vapours, now! Hence! Good guests, I say, right hypocrites, good gluttons. In, and set a couple o' pigs o' the board, and half a dozen of the biggest bottles afore 'em . . . I do not love to hear innocents abused. Fine ambling hypocrites! and a stone-puritan with a sorrel head and beard – good-mouthed gluttons, two to a pig. Away! (III. ii. 101–14)

Knockem is proved right, though he considerably underestimates Busy's capacity. This is a relatively simple example coming early in the play where a series of judgements are measured against our knowledge of Purecraft's household gained in Act I. Later examples grow more intricate and teasing.

When Edgeworth steals Cokes's second purse he invents a particularly intricate scenario with Nightingale, who wittily sings a moral ballad against cutpurses even while instructing his accomplice as to the whereabouts of the money which the fool keeps taking out and changing from pocket to pocket. Overdo as audience has eyes and ears only for the ballad-singer whose didactic intent he much approves of; Quarlous, Winwife and Grace, however, watch the stealthier activity, commenting excitedly on the development of the action, its teasingly delayed climax and the expertise of the chief players. None of them takes a moral or social stance except to hope Edgeworth is not detected as that would spoil their fun; they do not even intrude when Overdo in his guise as Mad Arthur is arrested for the theft. They are noticeably prepared to excuse what diverts them and doubtless we as audience sympathise with that approach: it is a first-rate comic *lazzo*, far preferable to the earnest song it upstages in our attention.

It is not so easy, however, to determine a response a short while later when Edgeworth, suborned to steal the wedding licence from Wasp, comes insisting that Quarlous be present as audience to relish his sleight-of-hand: 'the act is nothing', he claims, 'without a witness' (IV. iii. 101–2). The self-consciousness of Edgeworth's set-up and the perverse choice of a legal metaphor to explain what he wants are quite unsettling and yet the situation is a perfectly logical development out of the previous one. In the first instance Quarlous chances to find himself a spectator unexpectedly so feels no pressure to take an engaged response; in the second case Quarlous has a prearranged part in the proceedings and a particular response – enjoyment of the artistry of a theft and laughter at Wasp's discomfiture – is expected of him. Given the cold fury of his attack on Edgeworth immediately afterwards, Quarlous is presumably unnerved by the whole experience, realising that his laughter is an expression of complicity in a crime. When Edgeworth subsequently addresses him as a social, because moral, equal, Quarlous is stung to the quick. Jonson has cunningly presented us with two kinds of theatre here – one escapist, one engaged – and shown that what largely distinguishes between them is the quality of the audience's response. Both episodes hold a mirror up to Quarlous's essential nature, but only in the second instance does he become conscious of the fact and then he chooses to evade the insight that is offered to him. Almost immediately he decides to act rather than to watch as that requires him to hide his true identity in a disguise. He only shows his face again when he has contrived to establish himself, as he supposes, beyond reproach or criticism as the wealthiest citizen on stage.

Quarlous has bettered himself appreciably by the end of the play; he has done so by trickery and deception and he is to consolidate his income further by a kind of extortion from Grace. Yet everything he does is within the bounds of the law: Overdo, Purecraft and Grace would have no means of redress. He celebrates his power by confidently instructing the Justice to act leniently in respect of the miserable offenders before him out of compassion for their human 'fraility'. All along the citizens have presumed they are somehow better than the fair folk: Overdo searching out enormities concentrates his attention wholly on them and ironically cannot conceive that Edgeworth might have criminal tendencies since he is sprucely dressed, has money and is generous to a fault with it. The pattern of juxtapositions within the play wittily questions such social assumptions. How does one discriminate between on the one hand Ursula eking out her tobacco with coltsfoot, fretting her cans in the filling, drunkenly misreckoning bills and devising a fluctuating set of prices for her pork to match the degree of longing in her customers ('If she be a great-bellied wife . . . sixpence more for that' II. ii. 106–7) and on the other Purecraft playing 'a wilful holy widow only to draw feasts and gifts from my entangled suitors', devouring instead of distributing alms, arranging marriages 'for our decayed Brethren with our rich widows, for a third part of their wealth' (V. ii. 51–6)? Both would claim they were merely making a living. Is Cokes, stripped of his possessions and most of his clothes on account of his stupidity, lost, and frantic like a child to find the security of his home, so very different from the naked Trouble-all he chances to meet, who is wandering in his wits and lost to all sensible discourse? How can one judge between Punk Alice, Mistress Overdo and Win Littlewit when they all appear clad as 'green women'? Talk of extenuating circumstances hardly applies! Lantern, as the voice of the puppet Dionysus, proves there is no essential difference between the player and the puritan and Edgeworth shows Quarlous there is no comfortable moral division between performer and spectator. *Bartholomew Fair* is, as we have seen, an intricate network of plays within the action of the main play viewed usually by self-appointed audiences who are often themselves in turn an object of scrutiny to another group of spectators. The boundaries between players and performers are repeatedly being confused: Overdo, for one, chooses to act as Mad Arthur to be, as he supposes, less obtrusive as a spectator. Finally Jonson organises matters such that the audience in the theatre sits contemplating an audience on-stage. Like confronts like. Jonson has contrived to make the art of performance a metaphysical conceit for the essential nature of every human activity on the grounds that all relations involve observation, insight, generosity – the attributes that determine the quality of the reponse we term judgement. Jonson simultaneously presents us with an image of the world we inhabit and dramatises the complexity of our relation to it to forestall too prompt and easy a response.

Generosity is the quality least in evidence at the fair – surprisingly so, since a fair is a place of Carnival which should induce a relaxing of tensions and a release from inhibitions. Normally comedies that deploy elements of Carnival end by restoring the characters to their responsible selves, chastened perhaps but with energy renewed. Not so *Bartholomew Fair*: we end with the characters shamefaced and confused at being discovered publicly to be irresponsible. Quarlous proposes a supper (at Overdo's expense, not his own: he will be prudent with his new-found wealth). Feasts often end comedies (*Every Man In His Humour* is one such) as a celebration of social harmony and general good fellowship. Again there is a significant difference here: citizens and fair folk will dine together; what they will celebrate is their shared knowledge of the frailties that mankind as compounded of flesh and bone is heir to. That might prove the source of generous impulses on which a proper social harmony could in time be based. It is a subtle ending, at once warm-hearted and compassionate yet – in its larger social view – cautious, even combative. Jonson never lets an audience wholly relax: genial Quarlous may be in master-minding the close, where his former self might have been cruelly malicious; but we cannot quickly forget his past or why he can afford a new tone of *bonhomie*. Sensing the full implications of complexities of tone is, after all, a proper test of judgement.

8
'The Devil Is An Ass'

A cursory glance through *The Devil Is An Ass*[1] will leave the impression that it is something of a repeat performance for Jonson. One's memory is continually being jogged by echoes of scenes, situations, climactic revelations, characters, even phrases that recall past successes. Face and Subtle were such clever and flexible impersonators, one can well imagine them several years on settling old scores, joining forces again, turning their attentions higher up the social scale and translating themselves now into Meercraft and Everill, a projector and his champion, even if experience has taught them to be more suspicious of each other than formerly. Then there is young Wittipol dressing himself up in the height of fashion as a Spanish lady as if tutored for the part by Epicoene. Corvino and his much-put-upon Celia are back with us in the guise of Fitzdottrel and his wife Frances who, though as dutiful as her prototype, is less averse to speaking her mind. Fitzdottrel seems a compound of several of the male characters in *Volpone*, being as enamoured as Sir Politick Would-be with daft schemes and zany enterprises yet, when necessity demands it, able to fake demonic possession with a skill to match Voltore's. Gilthead and Plutarchus are as anxious of the surest ways to get and stay upwardly mobile as Sogliardo and his son in *Every Man Out Of His Humour*. Lady Haughty's circle of Collegiates is clearly thriving still and keen to be recipients of the latest fashion in fucuses decocted by Lady Tailbush from ingredients that would have excited Eudemus' admiration. Critics have listed the many parallels with earlier plays

119

and mused whether the feat of creativity that went to the making of so original a comic structure as *Bartholomew Fair* had left Jonson's imagination depleted. If that were truly the case, one would hardly expect to find a work with the energy, wit and clarity of line that *The Devil Is An Ass* demonstrates.

Anne Barton has described Jonson as always being 'a basically accumulative artist, carrying over and elaborating similar situations, character types and groupings from one play to the next'.[2] This is true, though Jonson had not before been so prodigally self-referential; but this principle also seems to operate at a deeper creative level: we often find Jonson in his later comedies returning to technical problems he set himself in earlier work that he did not convincingly carry off in dramatic terms then for want of a properly developed invention. In *Bartholomew Fair* Jonson had finally triumphed in a comic structure that entertained audiences with strategies that also encouraged them to explore their own precise relation to the art of theatre by making them sensitive to their position *as* audience. Jonson had first attempted to create a degree of heightened self-awareness like this in his spectators in *Every Man Out of His Humour* by devising an on-stage audience to frame the scenes with their criticism of the progress of the action and an actor-dramatist who stepped out of this role to discuss his intentions with the two critics. The device proved too cerebral and too predictable, for want of variety in the handling, to induce the right kind of self-consciousness (relaxed, exploratory): Jonson's objective was all too transparent. By contrast in *Bartholomew Fair*, he prepares us with the utmost scruple and skill, teasing us into thinking ever more deeply about the relation of actor to spectator, before he finally confronts us, as audience, with our like in Lantern's puppet-booth.

There is an early play of Jonson's that technically bears a marked resemblance to *The Devil Is An Ass: The Case Is Altered* quotes as liberally from Plautus as the later comedy quotes from the canon of Jonson's work. Extensive allusion serves, as we have seen, in *The Case Is Altered* to heighten our appreciation of what in the play is *not* borrowed from New Comedy; romantic artifice in the plotting as imitated from Plautus is overworked to make other experiences in the play seem realistic by comparison. We are startled out of easy laughter at the familiar into an awareness of what is new, which is endowed with a remarkable clarity and immediacy. It was a sophisticated technique for a young dramatist to deploy and the evidence suggests it was too innovative for its time in its expectation that an audience would happily sustain an amused detachment from the proceedings on-stage: one learned spectator thought it all plagiarism; the majority would appear to have refused to see *The Case Is Altered* as anything other than a welcome exercise in escapism.[3] By the time Jonson returned to the technique of extensive allusions in *The Devil Is An Ass* in 1616, he had patiently taught audiences how to respond to his style of drama. To do this he had mastered a formidable array of devices to encourage spectators to suspend their resentment at being made conscious of the artifice of theatre. His new comedy brilliantly deployed the whole arsenal of strategies to keep the audience at a pitch of self-consciousness, attentive always to their proper relation to the stage action. Jonson needed to do this because his subject in *The Devil Is An Ass* is dramatic conventions and what they imply about an audience's moral scruples and modes of perception.

Jonson's openings are always powerfully suggestive of where a play will move intellectually – more an exposition of theme than of plot. Here his Prologue appears almost in the habit of a stage-sweeper, anxious to clear a decent space for the company to perform in from amongst the exquisites and gallants who crowd the playing area and 'force us act / In compass of a cheese trencher'. He continues: 'This tract / Will ne'er admit our Vice, because of yours' (ll. 7–9), which wittily draws attention to the elaborate dress and ostentation of one portion of the audience who frequent the theatre as much to be seen as to see. The tone seems genial enough yet it cannot but induce a degree of self-consciousness in these spectators singled out for attention, particularly since the expression hovers carefully between flattery and criticism. Not far into Act One we find one of the characters, Fitzdottrel, anxious to get through his affairs in time to let him slip away to join these very gallants on stage to watch Ben Jonson's latest comedy *The Devil Is An Ass*. Not only is he a quietly practising Satanist who cannot resist plays that refer to devils in their titles, but he also has a vast and modish new cloak sporting yards of plush and lace that he simply must be seen in. When his business proves pressing, he is desperate that he cannot escape even for the duration of a single act so that he might cause a sensation when he is 'seen to rise and go away'; he longs 'to vex the players and to punish their poet – / Keep him in awe!' (III. i. 435–7). Play-world and real world come perilously close to coalescing, so determined is Jonson that his audience accept his artistry as accurately reflecting the immediate tenor of the times. The implication is that, were Fitzdottrel actually sitting with the audience watching a play directly reflecting his own personal condition, he would still be too enamoured of his appearance fully to perceive the significance of what he is ostensibly contemplating. Which brings us back to those gallants being addressed by the speaker of the Prologue: he supposes they would be happiest if the actors were made of 'Muscovy glass' so that the audience 'might look our scenes through as they pass' (ll. 17–18). As the speech progresses it seems less physical space that Jonson is appealing for than mental room in which to work. 'We know not how to affect you', he ingenuously confesses, even as he sets in train a series of strategies to transform the dangerous self-regard he supposes in his spectators into self-awareness. Cunningly he invites the audience to give his play 'the same face you have done / Your dear delight, the Devil of Edmonton' (ll. 21–2). *The Devil Is An Ass*, he assures us, is written to a popular formula.

Up to a point, this is true. There was a craze for comedies showing demons hoodwinked by mortals with superior intelligences of which *The Merry Devil of Edmonton* was a notable example. Satan asks a pertinent question in this respect of the 'puisne' devil, Pug, he has agreed against his better judgement to send amongst mankind to work their damnation:

> Whom hast thou dealt with,
> Woman or man, this day, but have out-gone thee
> Some way?   (V. iv. 60–2)

It is Satan's next weary observation that pinpoints the precise difference between Jonson's comedy and the prototype: 'most have prov'd the better fiends'; he warned Pug as much in the opening scene of the play when he tried to quell the junior devil's ambition to visit Earth. It is odd in some ways that *The Merry Devil of Edmonton* had such a reputation as a devil-play, since the outwitting of Coreb, the demonic spirit, by the magus, Peter Fabell, is tidied away into a short Induction of some 85 lines and is devised simply as proof of Fabell's skill in the black arts which are then put to use to solve the difficulties of a couple of young lovers (her father objects to the match on financial grounds) and bring them to a state of happy wedlock. The play is essentially a latter-day romantic comedy in the Elizabethan manner with magic used to frustrate Millicent's father's scheming. The whole pressure of the play is directed towards securing a happy ending and no qualms are expressed about using devil-given powers to achieve it; both sides in the conflict make a questionable use of religion to realise their objectives (Sir Arthur places Millicent in a nunnery but only to give her time to prepare her mind to accept his preferred choice as suitor; Fabell transforms himself and Raymond, Millicent's lover, into a friar and his pupil to help her escape). Sentiment controls the development of an action which lacks ethical consistency and commonsense. Jonson's play also has its story of frustrated love but he confronts the issue in a far more clear-sighted and wordly-wise manner.

Ethical consistency is what troubles Satan in the scene which follows promptly after the Prologue's reference to *The Merry Devil of Edmonton*. What riles him is humankind's capacity to reduce evils that alarmed one generation into a subject for laughter to divert the next. He imagines the kinds of sins that Pug could devise would all fall within the category of merry pranks nowadays and his suspicions are proved right when his junior summons Iniquity as a vice suitable to accompany him to London. Iniquity's jog-trot doggerel in rhyming fourteeners sends Pug into ecstasies; Satan knows such a depiction of vice would scarcely pass muster with a provincial audience. Iniquity's imagination has seized up since he shared the stage in the 1560s with lusty Juventus. The whole opening scene plays wittily with hackneyed dramatic idioms as Jonson demonstrates how original inspiration quickly loses its power to affect an audience once it becomes established as conventional; the only possible creative use for such material then is as an object for parody. Jonson clinches his point when Satan shows Pug the man he finally agrees to send him earthwards to possess; the scene becomes a subtle parody of the opening sequence of Marlowe's *Doctor Faustus*.

Fitzdottrel, avid theatregoer that he is, has been much affected with Marlowe's play – not in terms of its moral argument and portrayal of the awesome consequences of selling one's soul for thirty years of unlimited power, but on account of its general idea of the usefulness of having a devil at hand to do one's bidding and find one hidden treasure. Clearly Fitzdottrel supposes that, like Fabell, when the time-limit agreed on in the inevitable contract with the demon nears, he will conveniently outwit the Evil One and live on at ease, prosperous and well-regarded. He has none of Faustus' intellectual, moral and religious anguish, no sense of blasphemy or sacrilege; he believes (tutored no doubt by other less scrupulous devil-plays than Marlowe's) that it is sufficient just to wish aloud for the devil for him to appear. When nothing wicked comes to his call, he consoles himself with the thought that demons have, perhaps, grown wise about responding so promptly to invocations, since in most such cases they are immediately sent journeying round the globe on paltry errands. Comfortable dramatic precedents wholly shape Fitzdottrel's imaginings and expectations. However, he will strike out an original path in how he plans to entertain his devil, should he ever get one:

> I would so welcome him, observe his diet,
> Get him his chamber hung with arras, two of 'em,
> I' my own house; lend him my wife's wrought pillows –
> And as I am an honest man, I think
> If he had a mind to her, too, I should grant him
> To make our friendship perfect.   (I. ii. 45–50)

Mephistopheles first manifests himself to Faustus as a monstrous image of chaos to test Faustus' power to gain control over his metaphysical anguish; Pug appears to Fitzdottrel as a dapperly clad man-about-town, a fitting, domesticated demon for the scenario his would-be master has just outlined. Given what we learn subsequently of Fitzdottrel's obsessively uxorious disposition and of Pug's intention of experiencing as much 'venery' as chance offers while he is in human form, this is a serious test of Fitzdottrel's commitment to his devil-raising project. Pug has taken him at his word and appeared 'in a brave young shape'; far from showing shock or dread, Fitzdottrel's response is total disbelief: 'Your shoe's not cloven. Sir, you are whole-hoof'd' (I. ii. 82). Presumably because there is nothing theatrical and sensational about Pug's arrival, Fitzdottrel refuses to believe he is anything other than a young blade, down on his luck, who happens to have the surname

Devil and who will work in his service for free. Only when he learns much later that Pug has made a spectacular exit from earth in thunderclaps, earthquake and clouds of sulphur is he finally convinced that he has had a genuine demon at his command.

Fitzdottrel's myopia is conditioned by the fact of his having no real sense of evil. The subsequent action of the play quickly demonstrates this. He has several times confessed on first appearing his fear of being cuckolded (except by the devil in the way of amity) yet hardly has he accepted Pug into his service than he is lured by the gift of an ostentatiously expensive cloak into letting a total stranger, Wittipol, pay court passionately to his wife in his presence. Admittedly he confines the interview to talk ('I forbid all lip-work . . . and I defend / All melting joints and fingers' (I. ii. 191, 199–200)) but the whole episode is still a kind of pimping and his wife Frances is deeply shocked by the impropriety of it all, particularly since he normally keeps her confined to her room as in a cage. But he has eyes only for the cloak and thought only for the figure that he will cut in it at the theatre, the envy he will provoke amongst the gallants, the stirrings amongst the ladies present. He acts solely on impulse without consideration of the consequences of what he is doing or making others do. The focus for the episode is the luxurious cloak which we are twice told cost fifty pounds; several times Wittipol's rapturous wooing of Frances is broken off to draw our attention to her husband standing there, smugly enveloped in its magnificence and convinced he has made a brilliant deal. It is a powerful stage-picture, incisively evoking the complete dissociation of Fitzdottrel's sensibility from the world around him. The devil is discomfited in this play not because of a man's superior wit but because of his culpable ignorance: Fitzdottrel has no apprehension of what constitutes evil because he is utterly devoid of any sense of value. Manly, Wittipol's friend whom he has brought along as 'witness' of the scene, makes two pertinent observations. When he first sees Frances, he exclaims: 'A *wondrous* handsome creature, as I live!' (I. iii. 28) which intimates a transcendent quality in the wife's beauty which Fitzdottrel is oblivious of and which his actions are setting at risk. Later when the agreed time-limit for the courtship is reached, Manly's response is 'This is the strangest motion I e'er saw' (I. iii. 258), which draws our attention through the use of 'motion' as meaning 'performance' to the originality of the scene we have just watched with him; and through 'strange' (which in Jonson's usage often carries a metaphysical charge along with the idea of the odd or eerie) to the soullessness of Fitzdottrel's marriage as revealed in the situation he has compelled Frances to experience and now casually bids her forget as if it were merely a 'wicked dream'. By the close of Act One two momentous events have occurred in Fitzdottrel's experience: he has registered neither as morally significant.

Jonson now wittily increases our awareness of how Fitzdottrel has no developed moral sense because he is devoid of any appreciation of value. The play abounds in references to the cost of things (well over sixty to precise sums of money) and the juxtapositions make for some telling insights about the values of the society we are observing. Wittipol's fifty pound cloak cost, we discover, almost as much by the yard in plush as the four pounds a year Fitzdottrel's manservant earns for his labours. Fitzdottrel's estate brings him in some eighteen hundred a year; once the shark, Meercraft, has ingratiated himself into Fitzdottrel's friendship and possessed his imagination with thoughts of the millions he could be master of were he to invest in one of the projector's many patented inventions, Fitzdottrel is charmed into handing over to him two hundred pieces (more than a ninth of his income) in the space of some thirty-minutes of playing time. The fact that Fitzdottrel keeps repeating his wish to attend the performance of Jonson's comedy later in the day serves to give us a pressing sense of the time involved. Forty or fifty pounds of this sum is to pay for a ring to be given to an aristocratic lady to buy her acquaintance and good opinion and gain the Fitzdottrels entry into a fashionable *élite*. Besotted with the idea of the fortune Meercraft has persuaded him to believe will soon be his ('What is a matter / Of fifty pound to you, sir?' II. iii. 108–9), Fitzdottrel begins to disparage his actual estate as 'a trifle, a thing of nothing' and for a whim is prepared to sign away his ownership of it under instruction from the lady after a brief introduction simply because he considers she knows great good sense in her talk about female etiquette. Meercraft supposes the Spanish Lady in question to be one of several assistants he has in train to help further his schemes. Were she indeed so, then Meercraft would have reduced Frances and Fitzdottrel to abject beggary – all quite legally – within a matter of hours. Meercraft *almost* succeeds: he is an enchanter with a golden tongue who can mould his victim to his will because

Fitzdottrel prizes nothing at its real worth. Frances, horrified at what she sees happening, has no legal authority that would enable her to intervene: on no grounds can she command her husband's respect. Our sense of the painfulness of her position makes this a far darker comedy than *The Alchemist*. There our focus of attention was kept firmly on the dazzling invention of Face, Subtle and Doll and their dupes were viewed largely on their terms; moreover the gulls were all isolated misfits longing to find a place in society and supposing that a better income would necessarily make them socially more acceptable. Fitzdottrel is a more complex figure as a gull: he has an attractive and intelligent wife and a decent estate which should properly exercise his care and responsibility, but absorbing self-interest isolates his sensibility, making him fair game to Meercraft and his cronies. Pug did not need to bring a representative Vice with him on his journey to earth; there is no question of reducing Fitzdottrel from grace to a state of sin: he all unwittingly *embodies* iniquity in his failure to meet the obligations, marital and social, that should define his identity.

So much Acts One to Three establish. Act Four looks searchingly at Fitzdottrel's identity in respect of his gender as he brings Frances to be tutored in refinement by the Spanish Lady at Lady Tailbush's salon. Frances commendably keeps her distance from the court gossip, the chat about fucuses and the catechising of Pug (now designated her servant) regarding the proper behaviour of an 'escudero' in respect of his mistress's lapdog. Fitzdottrel, however, hangs on the Spanish Lady's every word, intrudes on her disquisitions to complete her sentences and show how in accord he is with her views, and fondly falls in with the circle of women assuring them: 'I ha' my female wit / As well as my male. And I do know what suits / A lady of spirit or a woman of fashion' (IV. i. 344–6). In no time he displaces the Spanish Lady in leading the tattle. The other male characters have all significantly quitted the room, Manly (whose actions always suit his name) doing so in indignation as Jonson's stage direction informs us. At the precise moment in Act Five that Fitzdottrel learns that until recently he had a genuine devil at hand to do his bidding, he is actually faking demonic possession, frothing at the mouth and speaking in tongues under instruction from Meercraft and his cousin, Everill. It is their last-ditch attempt to recover the estate which they have been baulked of: the Spanish Lady, whom Meercraft thought a trusty confederate in disguise, was in fact the ingenious Wittipol who took advantage of Fitzdottrel's infatuation for the female personality he projected then to instruct him to will his estate to Manly in trust for Frances. Outmanoeuvered, Meercraft's hope is to get the will annulled on the grounds that Fitzdottrel was bewitched by his wife. The manifest theatricality of Fitzdottrel's performance with the aid of soap, bellows, fake belly and a mouse is patently ridiculous; yet it shows the extent to which he has become a puppet in Meercraft's hands with no will of his own. Pug was displaced from the centre-stage role he expected to play because his technique was wholly inappropriate: Fitzdottrel had no strength of character, no intelligence for him to seek to undermine; Meercraft and his crew proved the subtler devils in gaining possession of the man by exploiting his social and sexual inadequacies.

What Jonson has done is to take the popular devil play and, while observing its overall scheme, transform it into an apology for his own style of comedy as the more exact and rigorous in its depiction of the processes of evil. In *The Devil Is An Ass* the luckless Pug is not so much outwitted as ignored by mortals intent on pursuing their own complicated intrigues to get the better of each other socially, sexually and financially. The constant reminders of his former successes, *Volpone, Epicoene, The Alchemist*, coupled with a wealth of newly invented meta-theatrical strategies and jokes (such as Fitzdottrel's anxiety not to miss seeing the very play we are experiencing or Engine's persuading Meercraft to let Wittipol essay the impersonation of the Spanish Lady rather than Dick Robinson, who as leading actor with the King's Men was the projector's preferred choice, when all the evidence suggests Robinson himself was actually playing the role of Wittipol[4]) work to impress on an audience the urgency and relevance of Jonson's vision and artistry. Parody and a wittily self-conscious theatricality transform the familiar into the strange, and invest what are in danger perhaps of becoming the conventions of Jonsonian comic form and practice with an invigorating immediacy. The play itself demonstrates how an imaginatively engaged and vital dramatic tradition has to be in a state of continual renewal, and how every dramatist must master a technique for creating *space* in his audience's minds if his invention is to find a means of resonating fully in their experience. If *The Devil Is An Ass* achieved but this, it would be a great play; however, it offers yet more riches. The comedy is structured around two parallel plot-lines involving Fitzdottrel and his wife Frances respectively, though at crucial intervals they intersect and at all times developments in the one considerably affect our response to the other. The creative deployment of familiar material in the plot surrounding the husband offsets the exceptional originality of that concerning the wife. *The Merry Devil of Edmonton* is more romantic comedy than devil-play and the conventions of romantic comedy are what Jonson addresses in his treatment of Frances and Wittipol.

Wittipol had seen Frances once before setting out on several months of travel: returning, he has studied Fitzdottrel's habits carefully to decide a means of turning the man's shortcomings to his advantage so that he might gain access and pay court to her. This is not easy since Fitzdottrel expects his wife to find content simply in being dressed handsomely then locked away to behave dutifully in the upper chambers of his house. The scheme with the cloak gets Frances a brief freedom but for a reason and by a means that forcibly impress on her first the extent of Fitzdottrel's chauvinism and cupidity and then the contrast that Wittipol affords in being perspicacious, intelligent, thoughtful only of her. The device is the perfect introduction to the man and it engages our attention even as it does hers for the graceful panache implicit in its invention. Permitted to speak to but in no way touch Frances, Wittipol extols her beauty, sympathises with her condition which lets that beauty waste away unappreciated and touches with a tender tact on the sexual frustrations he knows must be hers in being wed to the likes of her husband. His every word speaks of his regard for the inestimable value of her person and her temperament. There is no doubting his ardour but the speeches keep subtly and relentlessly moving back to the temptation that she should show a courage, ingenuity and passion like to his and devise a way to escape the confines of her painful, soul-destroying marriage:

> Nor have I ends, Lady,
> Upon you, more than this: to tell you how love,
> Beauty's good angel, he that waits upon her
> At all occasions, and no less than Fortune
> Helps the adventurous, in me makes that proffer,
> Which never fair one was so fond to lose,

Who could but reach a hand forth to her freedom.
(I. iii. 139–45)

Denied the right to reply by Fitzdottrel, Frances has to watch
patiently while Wittipol sets Manly in his own place and proceeds
to answer for her, an engaging pun showing her how scrupulously
he will respect her reputation. He acts for her the exact character
he would dearly wish her to play:

> But sir, you seem a gentleman of virtue
> No less than blood, and one that every way
> Looks as he were of too good quality
> To entrap a credulous woman, or betray her.
> Since you have paid thus dear, sir, for a visit,
> And made such venture on your wit and charge
> Merely to see me, or at most to speak to me,
> I were too stupid, or, what's worse, ingrate
> Not to return your venture. Think but how
> I may with safety do it. I shall trust
> My love and honour to you, and presume
> You'll ever husband both, against this husband. . . .
> (I. iii. 195–206)

Frances's silence keeps us guessing how accurately this reflects her
own mind.

When we next see her she is voicing more of the outrage she
expressed to Fitzdottrel before Wittipol spoke. Clearly she has
been moved by the encounter and is anxious to let Wittipol know
this. Pug, who has been set to watch over her, announces that
Wittipol has called expecting 'to take / Some small commandments
from you' (II. i. 223–4); and she cunningly sends as reply a request
that he would 'forbear his acting to me / At the gentleman's
chamber window in Lincoln's Inn there / That opens to my gallery'
(II. i. 232–4). It is making a covert assignation under pretence of
refusing one. Wittipol hears, interprets and promptly obliges; he
has Manly serenade Frances with a song of his devising then,
taking advantage of the proximity of their respective chambers
across a narrow street, adds fond and sensitive caresses to his
renewed endearments. The impact of this second wooing is further

enhanced in our appreciation by virtue of the contrast it poses with a short sequence that followed hard on Pug's delivery of Frances's message to Wittipol. The devil, taking her words at face-value and determined to do some evil, tries to encourage Frances to think again, hoodwink her husband, choose 'squires of honour' and employ him as go-between; and, since venery is much on his mind, proffers himself 'for the variety, at my times', assuring her 'I do know my turns, sweet mistress' (II. i. 299, 305). It is a rude assault, terminating in a gross effort to kiss her; the words are crassly judged: phrasing, imagery (all to do with 'fine tackle' and 'fishing') and tone imply cruelly that a woman as finely dressed as Frances must have a rapacious sexual appetite. Pug sees Frances as a whore ('most delicate, damn'd flesh'), even if one as yet too afraid of her husband to practise what she desires. His presumption costs him a beating; out of revenge, when he discovers the real drift of Frances's message, he summons Fitzdottrel to his wife's gallery only to realise too late that, bringing the angry husband to interrupt the wife's apparent infidelity, is to support the *status quo* when, as demon, he should undermine it.

Pug's moral confusion and chagrin are hilarious but they pinpoint a real dilemma that Jonson has posed for his audience. Wittipol the lover is formidably attractive: his actions so perfectly judged, his poetic fire, his agile mind and resourcefulness, his ardour all proclaim him such; and yet the object of his passion is a married woman. Though Frances's husband is a dolt, the fact of his relation to her means that the only romantic consolation Wittipol can bring her is an illicit sexual union, however temptingly his wit may contrive to depict it. In *The Merry Devil of Edmonton* the whole movement of the play is directed towards achieving a marriage for the young lovers in spite of all set-backs they have to face; from Act One this is established as the necessary ending. Romantic comedy generally prompts such an expectation in the audience. Jonson deliberately calls on that dramatic convention in his portrayal of Wittipol: he excites our sentimental susceptibilities for a happy union as the neat and proper resolution for a comedy while continually reminding us that the only possible union in this instance would involve adultery. It is a beautiful demonstration of the power of dramatic conventions to get a hold over an audience's imagination and proof again, as with his treatment of the devil plot, of the need for an exquisite moral and psychological scruple in a dramatist's handling of such conventions. What Jonson's strategy does is to draw our attention increasingly to Wittipol's delivery: it is not simply his intensity of feeling but his self-assurance that wins our assent. His voice has a dangerous charm in the way it works on us, even as Meercraft's confidence is winning over Fitzdottrel's commitment to the most hair-brained schemes. (Jonson shifts us back and forth between the two groups of characters at this stage with unerring skill.) So complete is Wittipol's assurance that he is prepared even to dress up as a woman to get further access to Frances; as the Spanish Lady he can even captivate Fitzdottrel and charm him into betraying before Frances a covert effeminacy in his temperament. His handling of Meercraft shows too how he can search out people's most vulnerable selves with great precision. What we do not know in Wittipol's case is whether he would use or abuse the power that is invested in so deep a knowledge of others. The test comes when Fitzdottrel, ignorant of the Spanish Lady's real identity, hands over Frances with the injunction:

> She is your own. Do with her what you will!
> Melt, cast and form her as you shall think good,
> Set any stamp on. I'll receive her from you
> As a new thing, by your own standard.   (IV. i. 443–6)

Frances has hardly said a word to Wittipol till now, beyond expressing the hope that he will not think her forward in organising the interview through the adjacent windows. Alone with him, she speaks with a fervent intensity not of love or infatuation but of her despair. Listening to Wittipol she has recognised the intelligence, judgement, sensitivity implicit in his manner of approaching her and appeals not to his gallantry which would be a worldly application of such qualities, but to his chivalry, a more altruistic and spiritual application of them. She trusts him sufficiently to reveal the precise grounds of her vulnerability:

> I am a woman
> That cannot speak more wretchedness of myself
> Than you can read; match'd to a mass of folly
> That every day makes haste to his own ruin,
> The wealthy portion that I brought him spent,

And, through my friends' neglect, no jointure made me.
My fortunes standing in this precipice
'Tis counsel that I want, and honest aids,
And in this name, I need you, for a friend.   (IV. iii. 18–26)

This is the first transparently honest speech we have heard in the play; and Wittipol capitulates completely, using his quick wits in his role of Spanish Lady immediately to persuade Fitzdottrel to name Manly his heir in his will, so securing Frances's future under his respected friend's trusteeship. This is a happy ending of sorts, but one very different from that reached in most romantic comedies: here the lover proves the strength of his commitment, ardour and tender care by opportunely taking advantage of the framing of a legal document to protect his beloved's financial interests. It is the only decent expression of feeling available to Wittipol in the world of the play. Satan in the opening scene warned Pug of the need for super-subtlety these days in one's dealings with mortals: 'They have their vices there, most like to virtues;/You cannot know 'em apart by any difference' (I. i. 121–2). Wittipol's character is delicately poised in this fashion: the tension is finally resolved in favour of his better self when Frances makes an appeal to him out of the depth of her need not for emotional support but for social acumen and intellectual companionship. Had our predisposition for a romantic solution to the plot been satisfied then his alternative self would have gained dominance; it would have made us a party to a kind of moral escapism. Ultimately Wittipol chooses to act responsibly but to do that he must beat Meercraft at his own game and trick Fitzdottrel out of his estate. If Wittipol can do good by Frances, it is because passion has taught him to make himself a master of deception and an adept in the ways of a wicked world. When he pulls off his disguise in front of Fitzdottrel after the signing of the will and leaves with Frances under his protection, it is emblematic of his new moral and emotional maturity.

'Uncasings' are always startling in Jonson's plays: they tend to tear apart the whole fabric of illusion from which the play is woven. In *Volpone, Epicoene* and *Bartholomew Fair* the 'uncasings' occur within seconds of the end of the play and constitute the climactic denouement. Wittipol's happens while there is still the entire fifth act of the play to run. Frances's honesty invests her with considerable dignity and the courage of Wittipol's decision (he throws off far more than his costume and wig as Spanish Lady, divesting himself of a set of attitudes that previously determined his personality) gives him an equal dramatic stature and presence. In effect the play has reached its conclusion; all that remains is to tie up the ends of the plot. What Jonson offers us is a dazzling coda, in which he reiterates and with great brio works variations on the themes he has explored in the previous acts: the absent but much sought-after Ambler (Lady Tailbush's usher) finally appears and tells how lechery has lost him a fine suit of clothes; Pug, who had stolen the suit to cover his nakedness on becoming human, struggles helplessly to sustain the role the clothes have suggested to him, then, terrified of the vengeful Ambler, pretends to be deaf and uncomprehending to avoid a showdown; threatened with arrest for debt, Meercraft by contrast has sufficient presence of mind to cajole his accusers with promises of yet another bizarre patent, whereas Pug is sent to prison; Satan reappears at his most sarcastic with no compassion whatever for his minion's desperate need for help, but he eventually carries Pug off to hell, destroying half Newgate in the process; next we see Fitzdottrel with his make-up and props in his efforts to feign being bewitched; he is ably stage-managed by Meercraft, who with Everill persuades all Lady Tailbush's circle of socialites to accept the bogus charade as credible evidence of demonic possession. The lightning shifts of tone are executed with an effortless precision; scene by scene the action becomes increasingly spectacular; the wild farrago of activity is hilarious, but it is all patently *theatrical*. It certainly satisfies an audience's hankering after a well-rounded plot and the proper sense of an ending, almost to the point of satiety. Only the quiet confidence (the correlative of inner strength) of Manly, Wittipol and Frances can bring the bizarre antics to a halt. Just as the meta-theatrical strategies earlier in the play gave a pressing immediacy to the action there, so here the effect is steadily to enhance one's appreciation of the complex significance and the value of Wittipol's 'uncasing'. We are confronted by a frenetic world that is unredeemable precisely because it cannot recognise Wittipol's complete transformation (let alone understand or emulate it). The last act defines the nature of his change by implication and contrast: Wittipol once participated in this world, was even its most subtle exponent; but now he has no place there and our perspective on to that world has changed in consequences.

Jonson has played some fine games throughout *The Devil Is An Ass* with the audience's expectation that plays on particular subjects will follow set conventional patterns. He has mocked our romantic pretensions and suceptibilities and repeatedly exposed to us the levels of artifice on which the performance is constructed to quicken our sensitivity to what is pretence and what is genuine, to what is escapist and what is imaginatively engaged. 'Games' is the right word for the meta-theatrical strategies of this comedy for the tone and effect are always genial, light-hearted and expansive, however serious the underlying purpose. The play conveys an infectious sense of Jonson positively relishing his mastery of dramatic technique and his control over the devices of illusion that constitute theatre.[5] After *The Alchemist, Bartholomew Fair* and *The Devil Is An Ass* Jonson was to sustain a great freedom in his playwriting but he would never achieve the same exhilaration again.

9
A Second Interlude: the Court Masques

During the years that Jonson was perfecting his own style of comedy, he was also active in creating a wholly new kind of theatre (new, that is, in England). The court masque, fashioned out of aspects of state celebration and ceremonial, was focused on spectacle, and its scenic inventions and extensive use of displays of dancing demanded a special form of playing space: Jonson and his collaborator, the architect and scenographer Inigo Jones, introduced the proscenium and perspective settings into London. From the Christmas of 1605 throughout James's reign at Twelfth Night and Shrovetide and occasionally for royal birthdays or certain dynastic marriages they produced masques of increasing complexity and sophistication. As Jones's experiments in engineering produced ever more elaborate scenic marvels that seemed to defy the laws of space and gravity, so Jonson contrived wittier, more intricate scenarios to contain them. The intention behind the masques was twofold: to set off the beauty of members of the royal family and the aristocracy and their skill in dancing within a structure that would also pay compliment to the king both as host of the revels and as monarch of the realm. The lavish spectacle had a purpose that was philosophical, didactic and (increasingly in Charles's reign) propagandist, so its chosen mode was dramatic allegory. The masques paid gracious tribute to the king by showing him emblematic portrayals of the nature and qualities of majesty and true courtliness. That Jonson with *The Masque Of Blackness* should have started on this aspect of his career with confidence

136

and imaginative brio is not really surprising: as begetter of James's masques he was fulfilling an ambition to be the conscience of the court and arbiter of its taste that he had first sketched as a possible role for himself in the figure of Crites in *Cynthia's Revels*. It might seem odd that Jonson, the social satirist and writer of city comedy, should so clearly relish the chance to be involved in these courtly extravaganzas; but they offered him the opportunity to give dramatic expression to the high ideals and awareness of civilised man's *potential* that shape his other playwriting, but which of necessity have to be implicit there rather than openly stated. His occasional poetry had celebrated such values continually and displayed his own considerable erudition, urbanity and graciousness: the masque set a premium on such attributes.

The problem with allegory in drama is to find some semblance of conflict: Jonson's first extension of his basic form was the inventing of anti-masques – images expressing both scenically and in dance and mime ideas of anarchy and misrule to offset his presentation of emblems of order, good government and concord that define the watchful care and beneficence proper to kingship. *The Masque of Queens*[1] (1609), for example, begins with a coven of witches who are endeavouring to 'loose the whole hinge of things' (l. 145) by raising some monstrous 'magic feature' from the ground. The invocations will not 'win / Upon the night' (ll. 282–3) and they are suddenly dispelled by a real marvel (of Jones's creating): a vision of Chaucer's House of Fame bearing in its upper story twelve of the great queens of history and legend, women who have been an enduring inspiration for their strength of character. They are grouped around James's own queen, who is celebrated as one in whom 'all they do live' (l. 707). The flattering implication is that in her soul Queen Anne knows these virtuous queens of past eras and by her will and in her actions can make them manifest to present times. The stage picture is an image of queenly sensibility, where physical beauty is expressive of inner fortitude and conviction. This is a simple opposition; other masques in the early years begin to explore the idea that good qualities can appear in travestied or perverted forms that need refining before the true attributes can be appreciated fully. The solemn marriage rite in *Hymenaei* (1606) is disrupted by anti-masquers embodying humours and affectations as forms of self-love that have to be chastened before the union of bride and groom can be solemnised. The very title of *Love Freed From Ignorance and Folly* (1611) defines its shape and psychological significance, while *Love Restored* (1612) presents us with a world where Cupid is being impersonated by Plutus, the god of lucre, with disastrous consequences. There is an elegant fancifulness in this conceit but it carries a serious satirical edge to contrast with the later vision of Love surrounded by dancers representing his ideal attributes as honour, courtesy, valour, urbanity, confidence, alacrity, promptness, industry, 'hability' and reality.

'Visions' would seem to be the correct term here for the sudden, spectacular revelation of the dancers, magnificently attired and seated in rising, falling or turning machines of a breathtaking ingenuity which seemed to ride on water or float in air. To an age visually more innocent than our own, the effect must have been indeed magical, especially when seen through the flickering, hazy light of candles. Jonson and Jones deployed theatrical illusion to create the impression that the timeless had briefly been glimpsed within the time-bound. The stage pictures were evocations of enduring principles within the universe of which the performers and audience were the current, temporal embodiments. They were visions designed to inspire: images of absolute values to engross the imagination and be experienced as a state of heightened being. The masquers having displayed their virtuosity in dancing then took partners from amongst their audience and so beneficently shared their special status. Invariably at the close the masquers are called back into the proscenium from the dance floor; the visions retreat, dissolve, as Jonson insists 'They yield to Time and so must all' (*Vision of Delight*, l. 233). What is left is a memory and, usually in a Jonsonian masque, an injunction: 'The life of Fame is action' (*Chloridia*, l. 236). The stage has realised in the philosophical and visual dimensions what might have been deemed impossible; ultimately the vision becomes a challenge to the audience in the moral and social dimension.

This would seem to be how Jonson wished his neo-platonic conceits to be interpreted: as a conjuring forth by his and Jones's art of the *best* selves of his audience that they might know what to aspire to in the way of courtliness. Certainly this is the argument behind Jonson's defence of masques in his introduction to the printed text of *Hymenaei*: that 'though their voice be taught to sound to present occasions, their sense or doth or should always lay hold on more removed mysteries' (ll. 16–18). Given that expectation, Jonson must have been pained by the boorishness that audiences and performers are recorded as displaying sometimes at these events (Orazio Brusino of the Venetian Embassy was disgusted at the wanton destruction by the courtiers of a banquet set out with sweetmeats in glass dishes after the performance of *Pleasure Reconciled To Virtue*; several times the set was torn to pieces when the revels had ended; and it was not unknown for King James to interrupt the proceedings to insist on more vigorous dancing).

In the ten years that lapsed between the staging of *The Devil Is An Ass* and Jonson's next play for the public theatre *The Staple of News* his only completed dramatic work was a series of masques remarkable not only for their grand scale but for the way the poet set about investigating the mechanics of the form he had created. As with his finest plays in the theatre, he began to explore the nature of performance and of audience response to create the taste by which the masques should properly be enjoyed. The didactic content of the masques was extended to show how to perceive and interpret the 'removed mysteries'; the anti-masques in particular took on a new import.

The Vision Of Delight (1617) presents a variety of movements of the mind that may be defined as states of enjoyment: an anti-masque of monsters and mimicking pantaloons evokes the mind at play; then Night summons Fant'sy from a cloud; she presides over the rest of the entertainment. In a long opening speech Fant'sy lists an array of absurd situations, ridiculous cock-and-bull stories such as a disputation between a farthingale and a French hood, which are then represented by a second anti-masque of 'phantasms'. Next Fant'sy becomes aware of the Imminent Hour who, descending, summons Peace to instil a mood of rapt stillness over everyone; this impels Wonder to speak and express her nature, as the shutters part up-stage to reveal the Masquers in a bower where perpetual Spring reigns because, as Fant'sy informs us, of the benign influences that radiate from the king. The masque continually draws attention to itself as depicting the myriad acts of Fant'sy who poignantly instructs her young questioner: 'How better than they are all things made / By Wonder!' (ll. 160–1). The implication is that Wonder is naïve to take images for reality but that through a disciplined exercise of the imagination we can transcend the merely temporal. Indeed the whole masque is about the levels on which the imagination works and the need for discrimination as to the value of its various activities.

Pleasure Reconciled To Virtue (1618) similarly instructs in discrimination. A stage littered with a drunken rout celebrating Comus as god of the belly is cleared by Hercules who, labouring only for virtue, can see no pleasure in the pursuit of drink 'to extinguish man' and 'change him in his figure' (ll. 103–4). Mercury appears, urging him to find needful rest from his toil by exercising his mind with images of heroic virtue; he calls forth a vision of Daedalus, the architect, instructing the young prince Charles and his friends to see how even a recreation like dancing can be a discipline to help them subsequently confront the labyrinths of the world. The masquers are finally recalled to the Bower of Virtue where they were first seen with the injunction:

> 'Tis only she [Virtue] can make you great
> Though place here make you known.   (ll. 334–5)

When this particular masque was revived the classical superstructure and setting were abandoned; instead a group of loyal Welshmen appear insisting that, since the object of the piece is to praise the heir and Charles is now Prince of Wales, the mountain scenery should be of Craig Eryri not Mount Atlas and they proceed to give a demonstration of folk dancing. Jones dressed these characters in very dated attire and an audience might tend in viewing them as the anti-masque to be somewhat superior and patronising, but the instructions to the dancers in the masque which follows seem now like advice to the young aristocrats that they submit to the disciplines of heroic virtue to make them merit such simple-hearted, patriotic devotion.

Versions of these themes recur throughout the remaining masques composed for James's reign. *News From The New World* (1620) shows the reception of an announcement that Jonson has returned from an expedition to the Moon with his muse. The anti-masque is taken up with literal-minded individuals thirsting for gossip about ways of life on another planet; they are teased with nonsense by two heralds before Jonson's poetic vision is realised for the benefit of the discerning. *The Masque Of Augurs* (1622),

Time Vindicated (1623) and *Neptune's Triumph* (1624) all start significantly within Whitehall Palace itself as if, like the strategies opening *The Devil Is An Ass*, to force on the audience a sense of pressing immediacy. *Augurs* has a bunch of citizens break into the court buttery intent on offering their own masque to the king: dancing bears are followed by Vangoose, a showman, who promises through his magic glasses to reveal a salacious vista of the Turkish court and harem, but things go wrong and he summons up instead a world peopled with distracted pilgrims, frantic of gesture at having lost 'the light'. Apollo descends as god of inspiration, brings forth a vision of augurs from the antique world, and instructs them through the intricacies of the dance in the art of divination for the king's serious understanding. It is a profound defence of the art of masque and its spectacle as working through symbols for an audience's enlightenment. So too is *Time Vindicated To Himself And To His Honours*. Here Fame is first seen beseiged by curious persons, all eyes, ears and noses, looking for novelty, noise and distraction. They idolise a lewd satyr whom they see as representing real liberty and relish his satiric art because it is covert and a venting of spleen. Though promised by Fame a vision of the golden age of Saturn, they are quickly contented with participating in this saturnalia. The time-wasters who are time-bound are replaced by the masque, which embodies how time can be transcended through questing for and cherishing fame. The dancers are the votaries of Diana the huntress, who at the conclusion recalls them to her service to learn further how through her chastening discipline 'to keep soft Peace in breath' by killing vices since 'they are your wildest beasts' (ll. 485 and 489).

Neptune's Triumph For The Return Of Albion daringly begins with the poet himself in anxious converse with the palace cook about his problems with the ensuing masque. The chef clearly thinks his own the superior art and counters all the poet's problems about staging a sea-triumph with thoughts of how readily he could realise it all in his kitchen:

> I would have had your isle brought floating in now
> In a brave broth and of a sprightly green,
> Just to the colour of the sea, and then
> Some twenty sirens singing in the kettle,
> With an Arion mounted on the back

Of a grown conger, but in such a posture
As all the world should take him for a
   dolphin. . .   (ll. 148–54)

He can even heighten his clients' taste with an *olla podrida*, a
broth in which the ingredients (they form an anti-masque) boiling
together are all *rotten*. In a way this bears no relation whatsoever
to the masque which follows with its perspectives of Ocean's
underwater palace and painted vistas of the royal fleet in harbour,
except that it dramatises the poet's concern to be rightly
understood: his spectacles are more than ingenious displays like
the cook's to tempt an audience's jaded appetite. Granted a cook's
skill has its own degree of wit and invention, but skill lacks vision.
The poet's anxiety is a conscientious fear that his art is not
adequate to convey the full extent of his inspiration.

   Through the range of these late Jacobean masques Jonson has
moved from showing the audience its proper participatory role to
sharing with that audience in some humility his scruple in devising
strategies to woo them into the complete response he requires of
them for his art. The appeal is repeatedly for an alert spectator
attentive to the demands of his own role within the scheme of the
performance: only then can the spectator be said truly to have had
a vision. *Neptune's Triumph* is an invaluable portrayal of the
workings of the poetic mind. Though designed for Twelfth Night
1624, the masque was not performed because of a dispute over
precedence amongst the ambassadors invited. At Shrovetide *The
Fortunate Isles And Their Union* was staged using much of the text
and most of the designs for the abandoned masque; the dialogue
of the poet and the cook was, however, replaced with a less
challenging anti-masque about a fool's longing for Rosicrucian
enlightenment. The long-standing collaboration of Jonson and
Jones had for some years known considerable and aggravating
tensions, largely over the issue of who was the true begetter of
these court spectacles, poet or architect-engineer. Behind the
superficial wrangles lay a more serious conflict between differing
philosophies of the art of masque-making, which may account for
Jonson's increasing concern over these last years of James's
reign to devise meta-theatrical strategies that render the sensitive
spectator conscious of the experience he is undergoing. The anti-
masques (always more heavily Jonson's contribution than Jones's)

seem to be questing for ways of expressing a personal defence of the genre, defining the moral, social and political perspectives from which the ensuing masque is to be seen and judged. Jonson's stance was didactic, critical, admonitory; Jones's preference was for the celebratory, the supportive, even the frankly flattering to deduce from later examples accomplished without Jonson's help. Did the scenographer see himself arraigned in *Neptune's Triumph* in the role of the cook and there found wanting as one who could perhaps create marvels but who needed a poet to give his devices purpose and subtlety of meaning? After Charles's succession, Jonson and Jones collaborated only twice more (on *Love's Triumph Through Callipolis* and *Chloridia*, the king's Twelfth-Night masque and the queen's Shrovetide masque respectively for 1631). Subsequently Jones took on himself the whole task of devising these court entertainments and their nature changed significantly in consequence: statement was conveyed increasingly by visual means; the literary content was reduced and confined chiefly to the lyrics of the songs; the anti-masques lost the teasing intellectual complexities of Jonson's invention and became simply images of anarchy and misrule. As Stephen Orgel has shown succinctly in *The Illusion of Power*,[2] Jones's vision and artistry embraced what for the Court were to prove dangerous simplicities, for all their intellectual pretension – a criticism one could never level against Jonson's compositions in this genre. Jonson meanwhile returned to playwriting; his late comedies take a noticeably detached stance towards the masque and scenic theatre.

10
Caroline Jonson

Masques are quintessentially a coterie drama. Composing them regularly for a select few with the express aim of reflecting that audience's potential to realise a better, even best self gave Jonson opportunities to study at specially close quarters the relation between stage and spectator established through the art of performance, particularly since the masque deployed various devices to blur the boundaries between actor and audience. The four plays and the three completed acts of a fifth that Jonson wrote between 1626 and his death are in a diverse range of styles: allegory, farce, high comedy, pastoral. The physical seizure that afflicted him in 1628 in no way robbed him of his innovatory skills; if anything, the freedom he seems to have found in his mastery of dramatic form in the writing of *Bartholomew Fair* and *The Devil Is An Ass* grew stronger; there seemed to be no style (even that of Shakespearean romantic comedy) he could not turn his hand to and invest with his own characteristic qualities and tone. Though diverse in subject-matter, the last five plays convey the sense of being a group, much as his satirical comedies did earlier in his career. Anne Barton has glowingly defended the plays against Dryden's dismissal of them as Jonson's 'dotages' by tracing through them a developing and creative nostalgia for the literary and dramatic achievements of the Elizabethan era which, in contrast with Caroline England, came to represent for the dramatist a Golden Age that he had lived through without fully realising the fact. Jonson's personal revaluing of the past exactly captured a

144

prevailing mood of the times, as political unease slowly gravitated towards unrest: astute and sensitive minds went 'harking back to Elizabeth' for reassurance that a stable community could be a potent social reality.[1] Masques also celebrate the concept of an ordered world in terms of their dramatic rhetoric. In all the late plays Jonson incorporates ideas, subject-matter, elements of style, verse techniques from masques he composed for James and Charles; he even on occasion transposes whole speeches from them into new situations.[2] Reconciliation is a theme that recurs throughout the plays and it would seem as if in composing them Jonson was seeking to find means of reconciling his own two modes of dramatic expression and explore what years of conceiving masques might contribute to his mature comic vision and practice. Transformation from the chaotic world of the anti-masque to the harmonious, all-embracing serenity of the masque proper was the essential process of the court entertainment. Transformations had occurred as 'uncasings' throughout Jonson's major comedies, but not until Wittipol's in *The Devil Is An Ass* had the experience conveyed ideas of change, growth, moral betterment. The Caroline comedies all build on that innovation.

Given Jonson's capacity to delight us with the wholly unexpected in his final acts, it would be unwise to read too much into his last unfinished work, *The Sad Shepherd*.[3] As it stands it sets up tensions between a charmed world akin to masque and elements that are deliberately and wantonly disruptive. The opening stage directions show that Jonson clearly envisaged performance at court before painted scenery evoking Sherwood Forest with a distant prospect through trees of 'hills, valleys, cottages, a castle, river pastures, herds, flocks'.[4] This, interestingly, implies performance at a remove from the audience behind a proscenium arch; and it is a remote idyllic world to which the action introduces us, compounded of various literary depictions of the Golden Age. Robin Hood, Maid Marion and their band of green men are culled from folk-lore, legend and Whitsun festivities (and early Elizabethan comedy) as representatives of a carefree innocence and a relaxed society untroubled by punitive feudal law; to them as their guests in Sherwood come shepherds and shepherdesses drawn from the traditions of pastoral and Arcadian romance; they are to feast together in a glade decorated with garlands of flowers to celebrate their being wholly at one with nature. A witch, Maudlin, with the magical aid of Puck-Hairy (Robin Goodfellow) abducts Earine, one of the shepherdesses, in circumstances which leave her lover Aeglamour (the Sad Shepherd) supposing her drowned. Earine is imprisoned in an oak and released only to be subjected to wooing in the crudest fashion by Maudlin's son, Lorel, who in exasperation at her refusals threatens rape. Maudlin dresses her daughter, Douce, in Earine's clothes and bids her cause shock and confusion amongst the pastoral folk by strolling thus habited in their company. The witch transforms herself into Maid Marion's double and orders Robin's men to carry the great stag they have hunted for the feast to Maudlin as a gift; when they protest, she is by turns imperious, shrill, satirical and snobbish; this subsequently causes strife between Robin and the wholly innocent, *real* Marion.

Unfortunately, what is not clear from the text is how Jonson envisaged staging Maudlin's metamorphosis into Marion. Elaborate costume-changes for the Maudlin-actor would seem unlikely, given the extreme speed with which the performer is required to alternate between self and persona in the final scene of Act Three. The neater way would be to exploit the device of doubling, with the Marion-actor playing both versions of her self, the difference between them being defined by subtleties of stance and vocal tone. This would make for a particularly arresting effect at the end of the opening act when the first of these changes occurs; the audience has not yet been introduced to the character Maudlin (she will not appear until the next act to explain her scheming and her ability to 'Take any shape upon her, and delude / The senses best acquainted with their owners!' II. i. p. 649) so they are suddenly confronted by the shocking sight of the supposedly amorous Marion turning shrewishly on Robin, which leaves them as perplexed as he is. Setting, tone, the expectant celebratory mode, even Aeglamour's contrasting mood when he is first seen indulging a pensive, romantic melancholy as proof of his enduring love, would all match a courtly Caroline audience's sense of a fit decorum in masque. Yet the play is starting where a masque should properly end. Far from being dispelled, anarchic elements begin to intrude on the settled contentment until the mood evoked by the painted scenery wholly belies the tenor of the action being played out before it.

What Jonson seems to be doing is confronting a timeless, mythical place of perpetual summer and easy affability with the reality of nature (Robin Goodfellow is an earth-spirit) as subject to change and flux. This inevitably has concomitant effects on human nature which becomes a prey to moodiness of temper, the process of ageing and the onset of grief. The emotional tone of the play is steadily complicated as voices increasingly express pangs of longing, frustration, lust. Maudlin's transformation into Marion is maliciously designed to poison Robin and Marion's affection ('I'll grow to your embraces, till two souls/Distilled into kisses through our lips/Do make one spirit of love' I. ii. p. 646) by causing him to doubt his trust in her. Maudlin shows him (if the supposition about staging the character-change is accurate) an illusory image of his beloved as an actress, a creature of shifting moods, who is troubling because clearly skilled at plausible deception. The sight indeed momentarily rocks Robin's self-confidence. In Act Two Maudlin instructs Douce that she will only be able to recognise her mother by 'this browder'd belt with characters' that she is wearing, since 'ye may meet me/In mony shapes today' (II. p. 652), which suggests that Marion is not the only character in the play who is to be impersonated as a travesty of her true self. The extract ends with Robin, his faith in Marion as yet unshaken, seizing possession of the belt that is the source of Maudlin's powers. What complications were to ensue from his owning a magic talisman whose gifts he hardly suspects it is impossible to gauge, except that (to judge by the Prologue's promises) much mirth was planned to suffuse the pastoral.

The Sad Shepherd seems designed to expose the limitations of masque as distinct from drama. Ironically the scenery remains *fixed*, the backcloth or shutters becoming increasingly inappropriate to an action where character is what undergoes transformation. Far more evocative scene-painting is achieved by the power of language to work on an audience's imaginations as in Aeglamour's description of the River Trent where he believes Earine lies drowned or Alken's of the 'gloomy dimble' where Maudlin dwells. The more the characters suffer the pains, insecurities, confusions that flesh is heir to and the more that perplexing circumstance causes them to doubt or to reaffirm their self-assurance, so the more human they become and the fitter material for drama. *The Sad Shepherd* is a highly sophisticated treatment of fantasy that scrupulously avoids becoming indulgent or escapist.

The masque is fundamentally an allegorical mode, defining

through the union of characters whose status is emblematic the composition of the regal and aristocratic mind: joy is expressed in the transcending of all divisive, self-centred potential and the achievement of an Olympian serenity, detachment and compassion. *The Staple of News*[5] adapts that allegorical mode to define the composition of the citizen's mind as possessing not the responsibilities of rule but the responsibilities attendant on the acquisition of wealth. Masque fuses with city comedy to create a highly original form of drama. Jonson pointed up the innovation in what he was doing by reviving the device (that he had last used in *Every Man Out Of His Humour*) of an on-stage group of spectators who comment between the acts on the development of the action and the handling of the characters. This time a bevy of gossips are the mediators between us and the stage, prone always to miss the point because too set in their expectations of drama: they bemoan the lack of a decent fool or a devil (one claims to have seen *The Devil Is An Ass* but has totally misunderstood its argument about the super-subtle ways in which vice is manifest in the contemporary world); they admire the vicious characters because of the way they dress or talk; and are convinced at every point that they know how the action will develop, having seen its like before. They want the familiar, think they are being offered it and dismiss it as dull and predictable because it does not surprise them. Their gravest error is to respond to the play as if the only possible mode for drama were realism. Mistress Tattle, for example, observes the third act which shows the Staple itself in operation (it is a public office established for the gleaning and purveying of news as a saleable commodity; most of the items that we hear are arrant nonsense) and judges it pathetic in comparison with the gossip she can pick up in a morning's stroll. She also questions why Jonson should hold the subject up for ridicule when in her opinion having an ear for scandal and a talent for polishing and elaborating on it in the retelling passes the time so very conveniently. Ironically the right application of the mind is in large measure Jonson's subject; and he does give a shape to his argument and allegory by deploying a well-known narrative as outline for his plot: the parable of the Prodigal Son. Typically, however, it is the changes Jonson makes in the familiar story that carry much of his meaning, and these pass the gossips by, unnoticed. The women are a hilarious strategy for showing an audience how *not* to interpret the significance of what they are watching and a far more inventive framework for keeping his spectators in a state of detached and witty appraisal than Jonson achieved earlier with Mitis and Cordatus.

Pennyboy Junior has acquired his fortune by inheritance not deed of gift after his father's unexpected demise. We encounter him on the morning he comes into his maturity: 'The powers of one and twenty, like a tide, / Flow in upon me, and perceive an heir / Can conjure up all spirits in all circles' (I. ii. 135–7). He is eagerly sought out by tradesmen wishing to dun him and upper-class parasites and toadies intent on living off him while despising him for his gauche foolhardiness. Junior has an uncle, Pennyboy Senior, who has amassed great wealth by usury and a miserly life (he sells the presents of lavish food his creditors send him and dines 'like an old hoary rat with mouldy pie-crust'; he berates a porter for spending sixpence to treat a friend to sack, viewing it as wanton extravagance beside the compound interest it would have attracted had he invested it for the likely duration of his life). Senior's wealth is represented by the heroine, Clara Aurelia Pecunia, whom he has kept under strict guard but whom he now loans out under his nephew's protection. It is with the arrival of Pecunia that the allegorical mode becomes evident. In the parable the Prodigal Son squanders his birthright in consorting with gamblers, wastrels and whores and is forced to live like a beggar. Pennyboy Junior makes his companions a motley crew of 'court-beggars': an emissary, a doctor, a sea-captain, a poetaster, a pursuivant of the College of Arms, and the Master of the News Agency, the Staple, who form a company of Jeerers. Ignominious themselves, they exercise their minds by denigrating anyone they consider superior; they are 'like lepers showing one another their scabs / Or flies feeding on ulcers' (IV. i. 35–6). Junior entertains Pecunia at the Staple and in their company with considerable largesse; he does not go with whores, but rather is prodigal with Pecunia's favours, giving her up freely to be kissed by all the company.[6] In the parable the son returns abject and repentant to be welcomed by a compassionate, understanding father. Junior was brought news of his father's death by an old Canter or gypsy for whose rugged, frank manner he develops a great liking. Canter is admitted to the company in the role of Junior's all-licensed fool, who scoffs at the imbecilities and trivia on which they waste their time; he is derided by the Jeerers but defended by Junior: 'Nay I do cherish virtue though in rags' (IV. iv. 61). The Canter asserts that all the Jeerers are in their several professions mouthers of cant and proceeds to satirise their various styles of jargon. When Junior finds this a source of joy rather than disgust, the Canter throws off his rags to reveal himself as Junior's father, who has played this trick on him to test how sensibly he will handle his inheritance. He bids Junior exchange his gaudy apparel for the cloak of rags and takes Pecunia into safe keeping.

Once again in Jonson a dramatic throwing off of disguise, an 'uncasing', draws the thematic strands of the play together in a potent image. The prologue advised that the play was designed for listeners rather than viewers; if we have listened carefully to the Canter (which the Gossips signally fail to do) we should long since have begun to suspect that appearances in his case are likely to prove deceptive. Within the company he pursues an idiom akin to that of the Jacobean Malcontent, but in his asides – and significantly he is the only character in the play for whom this device is consistently deployed – he voices a profound criticism of everyone else on stage. Intellectuals in the audience would perceive that Jonson invests the Canter with moral authority by sometimes giving him in these asides material translated from Seneca's *Epistles*.[7] The gist of his argument continually is to deplore the contemporary way with wealth: 'thrust riches outward / And remain beggars within' (III. ii. 241–2). He, a beggar without, is the one character with a rich enough sensibility to withstand the lure of the trivial which obsesses everyone else. The Jeerers are repeatedly nonplussed by anyone who questions their fundamental *characters* as states of being; the action exposes them as merely caricatures of men beside the Canter. *Listening* is the crucial response here on our part too. The Jeerers attempt to create a little dignity and stature for themselves: they give their respective callings an air of mystique by resorting to abstruse technical jargon, which, as the Canter observes, 'affects the sense it has not' (IV. iv. 75). Junior admits he does not understand it but relishes it because 'it sounds well' (IV. iv. 28). Tone and its relation to content have been steadily emphasised by Jonson as the play has progressed by a pattern of subtle contrasts: the Jeerers' malice is set against the Canter's public voice of malcontented railing and against his private authorative criticism; and the exact, succinct expressiveness of that mode is juxtaposed beside the Jeerers' attempt to summon a measure of authority through turgid cant. We have been urged to listen the better to discriminate. The Canter tries to educate Junior's *ear* and through that his judgement. The courtiers and professional men Junior has taken as friends are all travesties of their kind. Junior should learn how to detect a real gentleman. Failing in his objective, the Canter 'uncases' to deliver a palpable psychic shock, humiliating Junior by exposing the full extent of his want of perception and feeling. This father turns away from the prodigal, takes back his wealth and is anything but forgiving.

The Gossips, supposing this the end of the play, are outraged, then astonished by the return of the actors for a fifth act. We have already had intimations that Pennyboy Canter is not the only figure in the action who is more than what his 'outside' shows him to be. The Canter assumed a role for beneficent, educative ends and his impersonation was controlled at all times by a firm moral purpose. Credibly to sustain the pretence of that role he had to enlist the aid of a lawyer, Picklock, who has learned by the device to become an actor too but in the Machiavellian way: role-playing is his mode of promoting his own interests. Picklock was made trustee of the estate while Junior's father was supposed dead; now by legal chicanery he tries to retain possession of it, and to further his ends appeals to Junior's greed to repossess Pecunia as a way of alienating father and son absolutely. What Picklock has not banked on is the genuine transformation that the psychic shock has worked on Junior. In the days of his prodigality he allowed the Canter his voice in the company as the spokesman for commonsense, even if he did not then heed the advice. Junior has learned his lesson about not trusting to appearances and starts his reformation by suspecting Picklock's motives; he contrives to expose to his father Picklock's double-dealing and outwits the lawyer over possession of the deeds relating to the estate by cleverly acting as a *role* the character of foolish, self-pitying wretch that Picklock ascribes to him. Junior acquires maturity by developing the ability to act. This prodigal son has to prove his worth by showing he is sufficiently astute in the ways of the world to extricate his father from the legal tangles he is fettered by, which is to prove that he values the estate as much as his parent does. Prodigality is defined in the first four acts of *The Staple of News* as the futile expenditure of wealth in sustaining an air of self-importance; in Act Five the dramatic mode somewhat changes as Junior proves his character in action and wins his father's grudging respect: 'This act of piety and good affection / Hath partly reconcil'd me to you' (V. iii. 23–4).

The Staple of News is a very witty adaptation of elements of masque to reflect not the king's but the citizen's sensibility: the allegory depicts not an ideal state here, but a pragmatic and sensible one. The prodigal's father shows his son that one can only transcend a trivial and vacuous existence by cultivating qualities of mind that lead to a shrewd detachment through which one can manipulate the ways prevailing in the world to (one hopes) good advantage. It is the lesson Wittipol learned: how to discover, honour and safeguard one's integrity, which often requires one to *act* creatively. We witness a brilliant transformation in the play, but it is private and psychological; moreover Junior is immediately pressured into actively demonstrating his changed condition.

Masque served Jonson's purposes in *The Staple of News* only so far: ultimately character had to be tested against social circumstance. Jonson also appears to grow dissatisfied with the restrictions of working in the allegorical mode: the Staple itself, the Jeerers and the kissing sequence are well conceived; less successful is Pecunia's long description, to justify her refusal to return to Pennyboy Senior's care, of how he maltreated her, 'kept me close prisoner, under twenty bolts' (IV. iii. 33), which hardly accords with their first scene together in which he worships her like an idol and has her dress herself resplendently. Allegorical neatness and psychological verisimilitude do not always fit comfortably together in the play. With *The Magnetic Lady*[8] Jonson seems concerned again to depict the successful civic sensibility, but his dramatic method is here wholly different, though an affiliation with masque can still be felt in the preoccupation with a central, ordering genius, appropriately named Compass. The play begins by repeatedly drawing an audience's attention to Jonson himself as playwright. As in *The Staple of News* an on-stage group of spectators provides a framework for the action; two self-appointed critics, Probee and Damplay, are joined by a Boy-player who, acting as Jonson's spokesman, informs them that the new play is to explore humour types in the fashion the dramatist has been noted for since *Every Man In His Humour*, and which he has continued to revert to throughout his career. Indeed Acts One and Two do present us with a heterogeneous gathering of eccentrics, quacks and charlatans in the manner of the early satirical comedies. The Boy takes care to inform us that there is to be an innovation in that the humours in the course of the action will be reconciled. This is a characteristic Jonsonian flourish; so too is the Boy's advice about how the critics should approach the play: 'like a skein of silk', which, taken 'by the right end, you may wind off at pleasure . . . but if you light on the wrong end, you will pull all into a knot or elf-lock' (Induction, pp. 507–8). Clearly we must abide by the event and not indulge in unwarranted speculations lest, in our disappointment at not getting what we anticipate, we miss the delight and purport of what is offered. More startling is the sudden reference to Jonson in the dialogue of the first scene. Compass has invited the rough soldier, Ironside, to dine at Lady Loadstone's, whose niece, being of marriageable age, is attracting a swarm of suitors to the house. When two of the household, the parson and the doctor, pass by, Compass describes each of their characters with the detailed precision of a well-turned epigram. Palpably he is quoting from memory and, when quizzed about the authorship by Ironside, Compass admits that they are both by 'a great clerk / As any is of his bulk, Ben Jonson' (I. i. p. 510). (Jonson had published these poems previously.)

Jonson's strategy in devising as central character a man well versed in his own work is not immediately apparent. It endows Compass with authority and his pithy judgements of other characters justify our continuing trust. Compass has brought Ironside to the house in the hope that his brusque manner will raise the hackles of some of the suitors courting Placentia and thus afford a welcome diversion. There seems no malicious intent in this, nor has the projected scenario any sinister motive behind it, like Mosca's or Truewit's. The leisurely pace of the first two acts introduces us to what seems the relatively settled community at Lady Loadstone's, except that the situation we are presented with has its tensions in being in a state of deadlock: Lady Loadstone has chosen Practice, a personable young lawyer, as bridegroom, but he has declined on account of his affection for Placentia's waiting-woman, Pleasance; the other suitors begin bribing or otherwise inveigling members of the household to promote their interests; the bride-to-be fancies marrying Diaphanous Silkworm, the courtier, and bearing a title, but she cannot marry against her aunt's will without losing her handsome dowry; Placentia, moreover, is unwell; Compass, though in every way eligible as a suitor, is not proffering himself but using his quick judgement to advise Lady Loadstone. This plotting all hovers on the periphery of our awareness as Jonson directs our attention chiefly at character, especially Compass's accuracy of insight and his confident handling of others on the basis of these appraisals. Ironside is kept waiting offstage, held back from becoming the catalyst to effect change until we fully appreciate the need for action. Act Two ends with the characters going off to their promised dinner; Act Three opens in uproar: Ironside has finally shown his colours and attacked Sir Diaphanous for being unmanly and watering his wine. Having handled the plotting quite casually until now, Jonson changes his dramatic tactic and lets plotting positively usurp our attention with an apparently freewheeling spontaneity. Suddenly *anything* might happen.

Placentia faints, is found to be pregnant, goes into labour and produces a bouncing baby boy. Ironside is attacked and villified by everyone for his uncivil behaviour at table, only to be congratulated by all the suitors, once Placentia's condition is rumoured, for having saved them all from an embarrassing future. Compass chances to overhear a slanging match between Polish, Lady Loadstone's gossip, and Keep, Placentia's nurse, which reveals that Placentia is actually Polish's daughter and Pleasance the true heiress, Polish having changed the two cradles when the girls were infants to give her own daughter golden prospects. The two women privately settle their quarrel after the midwife finds a secret home for the baby, gives Placentia a 'caudle' to set her on her feet with all her strength restored, and urges Polish to pretend the rumours are all malicious and that Placentia merely 'had a fit of the mother'. Learning Practice's intention of quietly marrying Pleasance, Compass forestalls him, then exacts a public confession of his new wife's true parentage from Polish and the dowry from her miserly uncle, Sir Moth Interest.

Incidents culled from folklore, fairy tale and popular comedy go to the shaping of all this activity, which might seem palpable nonsense, were it not for Jonson's masterly control of the pacing of events and the sense he conveys that it is all growing credibly out of tensions intimated in the opening acts. The image that steadily emerges to grip our imaginations is of Compass as the still centre of the frantic movement. Whatever the development, he remains calm, assured, watchful, adaptable to changing circumstance. When he learns of Lady Loadstone's displeasure over the dinner-time brawl and sees that Silkworm is likely to challenge Ironside to a duel, he subtly works on the man's cowardice to calm him down without injuring the man's dignity further and has all but effected a reconciliation between the opponents when news of the birth makes Ironside the hero of the hour and thoughts of fighting are instantly forgotten. It might be supposed that this is anti-climactic, that a deal of stage-time has been devoted to an episode that just peters out because the play lacks a proper sense of direction. In fact the incident is part of a pattern that is established after Act Two: several times the action appears to be moving logically towards a particular ending which is then disrupted by a new turn of events – Practice's withdrawal from a match with Placentia; the brawl; the announcement of the birth; Placentia's startling reappearance in full strength. What impresses us is that each time it is Compass who shapes matters towards an ending that seems best for all parties at that given moment: he actively works to create concord in the community, deploying his profound awareness of other people's natures and attitudes to bring them into a willing acquiescence to the order he seeks to promote. He is never thrown by the unexpected, but skilfully accommodates it, realigning the elements in his overall design where necessary, and taking personal advantage of developments when they are likely to enhance his own social status. (He has affection for Pleasance but does not propose marriage to her until he discovers by chance her true class and estate.) Dauphine shaped the ending of *Epicoene* in a fashion that exposed him as a heartless cynic; his clever determining of the plot shows Compass to be an opportunist, but whatever reservations we may have about that are offset by his respect for Lady Loadstone's reputation, his imaginative daring, genial spirits and social awareness. The ending he achieves will allow most of the community to live on amicably together. Compass possesses the quick wits that characters in earlier Jonson plays have (Mosca, Face) but they are directed here at socially acceptable ends: significantly he never *acts* but works always in his own person. The fact that Compass starts the play by quoting Jonson's poetry with approval gains in resonance as the action progresses:

he is observed putting the values learned through study into action. The first two acts evoke Jonson's early style of satirical comedy and Compass stands apart observing it like a shrewd spectator at a play; called upon to participate in Act Three, Compass begins to let his judgement engage with his imagination in governing his actions. Much of Jonson's dramatic art has been preoccupied with defining directly or indirectly the proper relation between audience and play: Compass is the exemplary spectator – he sees through the anarchic follies and deceptions being played around him and comes at the truth of people's psychological and social conditions as a basis on which to fashion potential social harmony. Though there is no direct reference to the court masque, as there is to other aspects (early and late) of Jonson's writing, its values and function are implicit within the whole design of the last three acts. *The Magnetic Lady* subtly offers an *apologia* by the elderly Jonson for his ambitions and the range of his achievements as a dramatist.

Jonson's last completed play, *A Tale Of A Tub*,[9] shows his invention in no way impaired by his bedridden condition but building on the technical innovations of *The Magnetic Lady*. The result is a buoyant farce ('our ridiculous play') about Audrey Turfe's attempts to wed in the course of a St Valentine's Day. Her parents have chosen John Clay, a tilemaker, as spouse but the local squire, Tub, and his rival, a Justice, have desires on her too, not to mention her father's servant, Puppy, or Pol Martin, 'huisher' to Tub's mother. Though much in demand and eager to marry, Audrey is continually deprived of her current potential bridegroom by the machinations of a rival just when the altar or a parson seems in sight. She grows desperate:

> Husbands, they say, grow thick, but thin are sown;
> I care not who it be, so I have one.   (III. iii. p. 605)

Holding her (briefly) in his arms, Tub has his reservations ('The more I view her, she but looks so, so' II. i. p. 593) and finds her wanting in wit, but still goes in pursuit of her. Clearly the chase is all, and indeed much of the delight of the farce lies in Jonson's seemingly endless series of schemes to keep ever at bay the proper ending for such a romantic plot. Disguisings and double-crossings abound as rival outwits rival, while the local canon, Hugh, proves the most protean and ardent shape-changer of them all. It is a hilarious romp quite without the satirical or moral pressures that customarily give an edge to Jonsonian comedy; instead the dramatist shows great affection for his large cast of characters (nineteen speaking roles) as he sends them scurrying about the countryside. So tireless is Jonson's plotting and so wittily sustained on the edge of plausibility that one could suppose him capable of continuing indefinitely, but eventually Pol Martin weds Audrey with Tub's connivance. The day's events are treated with good humour by everyone (except a mournful John Clay, who is dismayed and confused at the apparent loss of his own identity more than at the loss of his bride, since in the course of the day he has been suspected of robbery with violence and of being the devil but is too slow-witted to see how this has all been part of his rivals' mad scheming).

The play might have ended there, but Jonson has prepared one final surprise: by way of an encore he recapitulates the whole plot again at breakneck speed in the form of a masque which the bride's father's fellow constables put on at Squire Tub's bidding as an after-dinner entertainment for the assembled company. It is not altogether clear how Jonson envisaged this being staged, but the masque seems to take place as a giant shadow-play behind a lighted screen with the venerable performers presenting recognisable caricature-silhouettes of the bride, her suitors and anyone else who chanced to get swept up in the intrigue. Medlay, deviser of the performance, gives a running commentary by way of explication. The masque is divided into five 'motions' which correspond to the five acts of the farce and we, as audience to those five acts, watch the former persons in that drama now transformed into an audience watching their own life played out in mimicry before them. No tensions prevail in this like those present in the staging of the puppet play at the conclusion of *Bartholomew Fair*: for five acts Jonson has united the disparate persons that make up an audience through laughter at the antics on-stage; importantly that laughter is genial and warm-hearted, since we are throughout conscious that we are watching a *tale*, a well-spun, if somewhat far-fetched yarn. Jonson is exercising his control over our imaginations as dramatist to bring a relaxed, holiday mood where previously he had frequently created unease. The on-stage spectators too are charmed by the artistry of what they see and forget the divisions and rivalries that beset them earlier. We watch the experience of theatre create concord as its effect, even while depicting an apparently anarchic farce. *A Tale Of A Tub* was Jonson's last public skirmish with his own rival, Inigo Jones (the self-important In-and-In Medlay, deviser of the show, who 'has a monstrous Medlay-wit of his own', is a caricature of the architect) and his last statement about the relative merits of drama and of the court masque: theatre in any form, even one as simple as knockabout farce, can create a state of social harmony; such an experience is not exclusive to the masque simply because it offers as its subject an allegorical definition of the constituent features of an ordered world. Medlay's masque depicts a chaotic society, but it still elicits a united response. In *A Tale Of A Tub* Jonson creates a state of concord in his audience's experience, then characteristically he contrives through the play-within-the-play to make them aware of what exactly he has done. Jonson will always have us understand our relation to the stage.

By far the finest of Jonson's Caroline comedies is *The New Inn*;[10] it is also the one that most intricately weaves into a pattern some of Jonson's earlier strategies relating to the nature of performance with his current thinking about the art of the masque. At the heart of the play lies a profound and original exploration of what is the fundamental subject-matter of all masques: the tension that exists between man's ability to conceive of permanence and his awareness of the law of mutability that governs his life in time. The characters have all come to an inn, The Light Heart, in quest of freedom from social restrictions; they engage in play but the roles they explore reveal more and more of their true selves, even as the wish-fulfilling scenarios of *The Alchemist* did. There is, it seems, no escaping one's innate identity except by a resolutely willed change. Yet if that is one's intent, how in a world of licensed role-playing can one's serious scruple be appreciated? Jonson establishes the basis of his argument with a dazzling ingenuity.

The host, Goodstock, is angry that one of his guests, the studious and melancholy Lovel, is so frugal in his habits that he belies the whole tenor of the establishment. But his temper cools when he begins to perceive that a 'light heart' is something Lovel devoutly wishes he possessed, being frustrated in love because of his own chivalrous disposition. He is guardian of the young Lord Beaufort and, finding he loves the same woman that his charge is wooing, has withheld all expression of his feelings from the lady. Goodstock discovers the apparently fastidious, disciplined Lovel is a man of intense feeling; the sensitivity and precision of the enquiries by which he learns about Lovel's case, coupled with the trenchant satire on current social abuses that informs his speech, inclines Lovel to the belief that Goodstock talks somewhat about his 'seasoning': 'it should not come, methinks,/Under your cap, this vein of salt and sharpness' (I. iii. 90–1). Neither is what the other on chance acquaintance has supposed him to be. Lovel's beloved, the Lady Frances Frampul, now arrives with an entourage of male admirers and only a chambermaid for female company. Lovel quickly assures his host:

> (Though she be very honest) yet she ventures
> Upon these precipices that would make her
> Not seem so to some prying, narrow natures.
>
> (I. v. 54–6)

Her immediate intent is to transform the inn and hold a day of Misrule for sport; there are to be elaborate dressings-up; Pru, the chambermaid, is to be queen over them, but the grand dress commissioned from Stuff, Lady Frampul's tailor, to effect her social elevation has mysteriously failed to arrive and she is being required to make do with her mistress's cast-off attire. Pru appears first in her servant's dress to Lovel on an embassage from Frances, requesting that he join their sport; she parries all his scruples about doing so in a fashion that implies she understands his difficulties, respects his ardour and honours his integrity. She vows on her own initiative to use her authority in the coming sport to further his suit by devising a means to prove both to him and, more crucially, to Frances that 'All that is born within a lady's lips/Is not the issue of their hearts' (I. vi. 67–8). Lovel believes Frances to be the kind of woman who 'out of humour, will return no love' and therefore, surrounding herself with admirers, 'doth practise on all us, to scorn' (I. vi. 152, 155). Pru suspects this is his view but considers she knows her mistress better. As with Goodstock, so with Pru: Jonson immediately challenges any assumptions we may rapidly have drawn from her appearance. Though a servant-girl she has a penetrating wit and a courteous (not servile) manner suggesting a ready confidence in her perceptions and judgement. Clearly neither Pru nor Frances are to be quite what they seem. Clothes may indicate social position but little about actual temperament. Jonson in all his late plays urges his audience to *listen* rather than simply watch; as appearances become increasingly deceptive in the play, how we hear the characters and, hearing them, how we interpret their actions, gains correspondingly in importance. Discerning significance in tone is essential, and Act One has taught us what our proper response to the stage should be.

Act Two introduces Lady Frampul, who demonstrates immediately her quicksilver changeability of mood: witty, excitable, tart when crossed in pursuit of her whims, quick to assert that she is a law unto herself when it is implied her actions might be misconstrued and open to condemnation ('as if I lived / To any other scale than what's my own!' II. i. 58–9). Pru, we see, can manage this wilfulness with an easy grace, her wit and invention saving her from compromising her own judgements, even though she is now being dressed for her role as Queen of Misrule. Of Frances's three suitors, one (Sir Glorious Tipto), though decked in Spanish finery and grandiloquent in his every utterance, quickly takes advantage of the idea of a day of social licence to gravitate to the servants' quarters belowstairs in the inn, where, despite appearances, he clearly finds his proper element. Here he can lord it over inferiors and keep up the pretence of being a gentleman, while indulging his taste for liquor, bravado and bawdy; he remains oblivious of the fact that at least one of the host's men, Fly, is merely humouring him in his many pretensions while quietly treating him as a fool. Who here has the superior wit and who is patronising whom? Neither of the other lordly suitors continues in the relaxed atmosphere of the inn to make Frances the sole focus of his attentions. Partly to satisfy Pru's concern for propriety and partly out of a devil-may-care wish to see what comic confusions might occur to supplement her fun, Lady Frampul with the host's connivance has dressed his young son, Frank, as a lady (named for the nonce after Frances's lost sister, Laetitia); and Frank's wild Irish nurse has been fitted with 'a tuftaffeta cloak [and] an old French hood' as Laetitia's chaperone. No sooner has she appeared than Lord Beaufort has eyes only for Laetitia and, being a 'light, young lord', is soon engineering for them to get private and amorous. Though Lord Latimer hardly takes his eyes off Frances, he continually makes Pru the close confidant of his thoughts and feelings. Once the sport begins, Frances is attentive only to Lovel except when either of the lords chances to speak of him. A pattern of apparent allegiances has been rapidly broken and new ones established that in at least two cases have achieved a level of confidential intimacy with remarkable speed. We have watched three servants be invested with regal or patrician dress; one character merely by virtue of a costume has apparently changed sex. Little within the original scheme of character-relationships has remained stable; disguise does not seem to be a necessary requirement for anyone wishing to find a new role to play; those actually in disguise seem to be more completely at one with themselves than previously, especially Pru. Throughout Act Two Jonson has affected a sequence of brilliant transformation scenes: but what exactly are we now viewing? Are these the characters' anti-selves briefly adopted in a spirit of misrule, or are they projections of an inner truth to self released in the suddenly relaxed environment? What is in sport and what in earnest? That is a question that begins increasingly to perplex the characters.

Act Two is a superb evocation of a world of shifting appearances. Lovel does not enter it until near the end. In his sober suit of black, he seems the one person we can securely place. Pru describes him as 'sad'; Frances insists on the epithet 'sullen'; but we feel we know who is the better judge. It is the more surprising then that, as her first act as Queen, Pru commands Lady Frampul, who is unsure how properly to approach Lovel, to kiss him. After her tender concern expressed earlier for Lovel's condition, Pru's action seems wantonly brash, a gesture of misrule in the worst possible taste. Lovel retains his dignity; it is Frances whose self-possession gutters: she kisses but in a manner that might suggest embarrassment, humiliation or might equally well be interpreted as imperious, even designedly rude: 'Do not you / Triumph on my obedience, seeing it forced thus' (II. vi. 112–13). Lovel is in an ecstasy of uncertainty. Appearances again prove deceptive. The episode was a cunning strategy of Pru's to make Frances experience what others suffer under the dictate of her will; when Frances remonstrates, Pru is adamant:

Would you make laws, and be the first to break 'em?

The example is pernicious in a subject,
And of your quality, most.   (II. vi. 128–30)

Pru now has grounds for claiming Lovel has a right of libel against
Frances for her apparent disrespect of his feelings and insists that
by way of recompense Lady Frampul be required to listen to him
plead the cause of love for two separate hours and reward him
with a kiss for each hour's peroration. Far from allowing the stage
to degenerate to a place of anarchy, Pru has cunningly redeemed
it by imposing her will as law, which permits her now to transform
the inn into a Court of Love. She assigns to each character a ritual
function and bids them reconvene with full ceremonial. Out of a
stage that matched the temper of Frances's quixotic mind, she has
deftly fashioned one that now matches Lovel's tenor of high
seriousness. Latimer is full of admiration, lauding her skill as 'The
only learned mother of the law, / And *lady o' conscience*, too!'
(II. vi. 193–4).

Lovel's disquisition on the nature of love is, as one might expect
from what we have learned about him in Act One, heartfelt.
Exquisitely judged eloquence, clarity of argument and urbane tone
intimate a passionate conviction in the ideas finding expression.
These are chiefly that 'we must take and understand this
love / Along still, as a name of dignity, / Not pleasure' (III. ii. 118–
20); moreover, since 'love is never true that is not lasting', 'no
more than any can be pure or perfect, / That entertains more than
one object' (III. ii. 197–9). We are privileged and know, as do the
Host and Pru, that this is Lovel's heart's truth. This allows us to
watch the impact of his words on his listeners. Circumstance has
required Lovel to reveal his most private self in public in a situation
where he might be expected to act. Lord Beaufort treats the
proceedings as another of Lady Frampul's charades and tries to
undermine Lovel's seriousness with a line in witty innuendo to the
effect that the proper preoccupations of the lover are physical. To
prove his point he shapes his sentences cleverly to justify kissing
Laetitia. His intrusions in no way disturb Lovel's concentration
on his subject or Frances's on him. Though Lovel holds the stage,
Pru and Latimer are more attentive to how his words affect
Frances: both know her to be flighty and a competent actress in
her 'sports'. Is she now pretending to be captivated by Lovel's
fervent idealism or is she touched by it to the quick and seeing

the possibility of realising a more mature identity in herself through such a love? Pru suspects it is affectation; Latimer is far from certain. We have nothing to go by but tone and imagery: there is rapture but it is marked by an insistent exclamatory note ('O speak, and speak for ever! Let mine ear / Be feasted still, and filled with this banquet!' III. ii. 200–1). Though Frances speaks of herself as 'changed' and penitent, the references to alchemy and romantic literature give her words a slightly mocking edge. There is a similar ambiguity about her calling Lovel a 'reverend gentleman', since he is 'somewhat struck in years, and old / Enough to be my father' (III. ii. 227–30). Is she toying with him or with herself, being capriciously enamoured of the idea of being in love? Or, caught within a process of change, is she trying to shed her old idiom and find one that conveys a new-found sense of commitment? The mistress of many moods could be finding difficulty in sustaining one tone as genuine. Interestingly Frances's speeches here are highly intimate, being in substance and manner what would normally constitute an aside, but Jonson (usually careful about such matters) does not designate them as such. How much is she lost in wonder to herself here and how much is she calculating an effect? Phrase after phrase is beautifully pitched between possibilities of interpretation:

> I could begin to be in love with him,
> But will not tell him yet because I hope
> T' enjoy the other hour with more delight,
> And prove him farther.   (III. ii. 232–5)

Pru's response is apt: 'Most Socratic lady, / Or, if you will, ironic'. Latimer thinks her 'serious' and Lovel that 'she dissembles; all is personated'. Yet a deeper movement of his mind impels him immediately to the more generous apprehension that Frances's state is more complex than he first suppposed: to admit the possibility that all is not 'counterfeit comes from her' promptly excites his consciousness to a pitch of ecstasy:

> The Spanish monarchy with both the Indies
> Could not buy off the treasure of this kiss
> Or half give balance for my happiness.
>
> (III. ii. 260–2)

It is a telling dramatic moment when the cautious Lovel dares surrender himself momentarily to emotional extravagance. As the court adjourns Jonson abruptly changes the mode to savage farce for a short interlude. A mysterious countess is announced and appears 'very brave' in a 'stately gown' of 'glistering golden satin'; she is accompanied by a pathetic individual she calls her 'Protection'. Merely at the sight of her Tipto and his cronies from the cellerage begin fighting over precedence in enjoying her favours; Protection is outraged, but the lady is far from displeased:

> I hope I know wild company are fine company,
> And in fine company, where I am fine myself,
> A lady may do any thing, deny nothing
> To a fine party. . . .   (IV. ii. 94–7)

Characteristically making no judgement on her but as a woman in distress, Lovel (offstage) in a deft display of swordsmanship quells the skirmishing, which draws the 'Countess' to Frances's notice as she is now studying Lovel's every move. The lady still goes unrecognised (though Beaufort takes her for 'a bouncing bona-roba'), but not the dress: that is claimed as the missing clothing designed for Pru to wear in the current revels. Protection is summoned and found to be Nick Stuff, Lady Frampul's tailor; it transpires he habitually dresses his wife (the 'Countess') in the clothes he makes for aristocratic clients and plays out with her a sexual fantasy in which, masquerading as her servant, he escorts her out of town to an inn where he pretends to ravish her in a private room. The court orders the wife to be stripped of her finery and carted to town like a whore with her husband beating a basin before her. After the high ideals of Lovel's discourse, the episode is a graphic reminder of what are ofttimes the worldly realities of love in practice: preoccupation with fetishes, calculations over rank and social status and obsession with the trivia of appearance. Pinacia Stuff enjoyed the role-playing because as 'Countess' she felt herself free of inhibition. These are the darker possibilities of a taste for sport and acting; the Stuffs are an exact antithesis of Lady Frampul's world, a travesty that nonetheless

compels us to study that world now with a keener discrimination.
When Lovel returns to the stage he is remarkable for being, as
Frances quickly notes, a still, calming presence 'after this noise
and tumult'; she seems wholly attuned to his sensibility and on
impulse asks if the subject of the second disquisition might be
changed from courtship to valour. This is a neat device to give an
illusion of spontaneity to Lovel's discourse; the new subject is
challenging in requiring him to speak more closely of the principles
that govern his way of life; Frances is asking for nothing less than
an analysis of his identity, which is a real test and proof of valour
should he respond, as he does, without hesitation. This time Tipto
joins Beaufort in posing a counter-argument, but both are quickly
routed: valour is shown to have little to do with vainglory, skill in
arms or reputation; Lovel prefers to define it as a complete honesty
to the self, a shrewd assessment of one's inner worth which gives
a fitting decorum to all one's social relations. The necessary
attributes of a man's valour are therefore in Lovel's view 'his
patience, / His magnanimity, his confidence, / His constancy, security, and quiet' (IV. iv. 132–4); once possessing these qualities,
such a man is beyond the 'soil' of rumour, contumelies, injury and
aspersion. Lovel, concluding, wins the acclaim of all his audience.
Frances has been so thoroughly engrossed by Lovel's ideas ('Who
would not hang upon those lips for ever / That strike such music?'
IV. iv. 142–3) that she is startled to hear his allotted hour is over:

> It cannot be! O clip the wings of Time,
> Good Pru, or make him stand still with a charm.
> Distill the gout into it, cramps, all diseases
> T' arrest him in the foot and fix him here . . .
> (IV. iv. 227–30)

Pru, however, supposes that the elaborate conceits are only
rhetorical and proof that her 'subtle and dissembling lady mistress'
is once more feigning to stave off giving Lovel his reward. Believing
that her experiment to bring Lovel and Frances into a better
understanding has failed, she promptly bids Frances pay the forfeit
of a kiss, then dissolves the court, dismissing it all as no more than
a play.
The effect is catastrophic. Lovel is shocked into the apprehension

that the high seriousness was pretended in order to make him a laughing-stock; for the first time in the action his self-possession buckles in anguish before what he sees as 'Love's ungrateful tyranny'; tone and phrase compromise the claims of both his discourses. Perhaps Pru is right and what we have witnessed has been only clever acting; even Lovel's seemingly invincible composure now appears to be a studied projection. He leaves the stage peevishly denigrating love as a 'vapour' and claiming he will go sleep, if the 'leer drunkards' in the house will let him. Left alone, Frances rounds viciously on Pru for failing to understand her in presuming she was jeering at Lovel: 'Stay in thy state of ignorance still, be damned, / An idiot chambermaid' (IV. iv. 313–14). The cruelty is unwarranted: Pru has been imperceptive, but we can at least appreciate the grounds of her uncertainty. Paradoxically our uncertainty about Frances's feelings is now resolved: exasperation and anger in her, just as frustration and dismay in Lovel, have finally revealed an intensity of passion. Both show a truth to feeling, when, hurt, they are least like the selves they seek to project in public. It is by contraries that we have found directions out, not by statements, however carefully phrased or judiciously expressed. Pinacia's crass impersonation serves by the end of the act to highlight the far subtler levels of the mind where role-play can exist, setting at risk the ideals voiced by Lovel in his disquisition on love. The fact that valour is defined in the second discourse as an arming of the self against adversity and pain is an admission of the likely impermanence of the values extolled rapturously in the first peroration. Nothing in the play has proved certain. In the masque *Pleasure Reconciled To Virtue* Daedalus, the architect of labyrinths, advises the dancers that life is a series of mazes and that the 'subtlest maze of all [is] love'. It is difficult to see how Lovel and Frances could thread the labyrinth they have set up between them in spite of their best intentions, or what dance could now possibly draw the action of *The New Inn* to a satisfying conclusion. Jonson, invariably a master of surprises with his final acts, devises one here that cunningly intimates various possibilities for a resolution without losing touch with his underlying philosophical preoccupations.

Act Four has given us in effect one possible ending: painful and near-tragic, where the lovers remain divided as a consequence of Frances's previously 'frampul' nature since Lovel lacks the daring to trust in her capacity for change; and the fact of that doubt challenges her belief in him as a man true to his stated principles. The only way out of this stalemate is for Frances to find the courage to speak openly of her innermost need (as Frances Fitzdotterel did to such creative effect in *The Devil Is An Ass*); and Act Five opens with Frances herself perceiving the necessity of some such action to 'take occasion by the forelock' (V. ii. 65). But she cannot shake off at will her own past temperament: instead of going decisively to Lovel herself, she is planning to send Pru as ambassador. To fit the momentousness of the occasion, she has dressed Pru in the gown stripped off Pinacia and urges her in her role as Queen of the Revels to command his attention. Pru indeed now looks resplendently regal but it is over Frances that she asserts a voice of authority. The catastrophe she brought about has clearly taught Pru much about Frances, Lovel and herself: with impressive dignity she calls an end to play-acting and vows she will speak only the truth. Her tone is compassionate but absolute:

> No I will tell him, as it is indeed:
> I come from the fine, froward, frampul lady,
> One that was run mad with pride, wild with self-love,
> But late encount'ring a wise man who scorned her,
> And knew the way to his own bed, without
> Borrowing her warming-pan, she hath recovered
> Part of her wits; so much as to consider
> How far she has trespassed, upon whom, and how.
> And now sits penitent and solitary,
> Like the forsaken turtle, in the volary
> Of the Light Heart, the cage she hath abused,
> Mourning her folly, weeping at the height
> She measures with her eyes from whence she is fallen,
> Since she did branch it on the top o' the wood.
>
> (V. ii. 28–41)

Frances accepts the criticism and Pru's further condemnation of her indulgence in self-pity. (Jonson's gauging of tone in this episode is meticulous.) This prepares the way for an ending centred on a quiet, tender reconciliation between lovers who can now afford to laugh at their former reluctance to embrace emotional commitment. But before this possibility can be advanced, Jonson unleashes a torrent of activity in which his favourite device of 'uncasing' a character is carried to a flamboyant extreme.

Beaufort, who had surreptitiously left the Court of Love to wed 'Laetitia', appears with his bride and practically strips himself naked in excited anticipation of proving his virility. The Host and Fly halt the couple's progress to bed and laughingly divest 'Laetitia' of wig and gown to reveal young Frank. Before Beaufort can get over that shock to his self-esteem, the nurse arrives frantic because Beaufort has actually wed a woman, since 'Frank' is in fact her disguised daughter. Appalled at marrying a girl he now presumes a beggar, Beaufort threatens divorce; but the nurse next 'uncases' and announces she is the lost Lady Frampul, Frances's mother, and that the much-transformed 'Frank' is genuinely Laetitia. In transports of delight the Host pulls off his guise as Goodstock and dresses in robes proving him to be Lord Frampul, last heard of as estranged from his wife and taking to a life with the gypsies for 'sport'. He draws his family about him, accepts Beaufort into the group as son-in-law and, when Lovel appears, gives him Frances's hand in marriage, since he privily knows their inclinations. Latimer refuses to let Pru accept financial reward for her services: asserting that 'she is a dowry / So all-sufficient in her virtue and manners / That fortune cannot add to her' (V. v. 143–5), he claims the chambermaid-turned-queen as his wife. Lovel, coming late to the action, is again thrust into a world of shifting appearances and is justifiably amazed:

> Is this a dream now, after my first sleep?
> Or are these phant'sies made i' the Light Heart,
> And sold i' the New Inn?   (V. v. 120–2)

Lovel's observation is precise: we, as audience, have watched such stuff as dreams are made on, wish-fulfilling fantasies that are transparently theatrical. And yet Lovel's tone as one caught up in the action is of *wonder*, not cynicism. In John Caird's recent production the last act excited laughter, but of a warm-hearted not derisive kind.[11] To an astonishing degree absurdity and high seriousness seemed inextricably fused. The far-fetched quality of this ending with its round of physical 'uncasings' invests the two earlier possibilities for a conclusion with a greater realism, where the 'uncasings' are subtle and psychological, a shedding of illusions to confront a painfully vulnerable self in the face of potential loss and heartbreak. But audience expectation of comedy is generally that it will conclude with the heart at ease: there is a hunger for emotional permanence. For much of his career Jonson criticised the tradition of romantic comedy and continually made audiences investigate the motives behind their expectations of theatre. Over two decades in his masques he had devised images of permanence, conscious always that performers and audience fell far short of the ideal worlds he depicted there. *The New Inn* satisfies totally an audience's expectations for an emotionally complete ending. (Jonson, be it said, carefully prepares the ground for all the revelations and reversals, except for the nurse's concealed identity as Lady Frampul.) The four previous acts have, however, shown us repeatedly how appearances are deceptive and so taught us to look behind the surface of things, especially at motives behind role-play. It is the number and rapidity of the 'uncasings' that create the effect of self-conscious theatricality: they are palpably devices manipulating us emotionally. Yet each of the transformations that bring the happy resolution closer actually acknowledges the possibility of behaviour that could just as easily prove emotionally divisive and tragic in its outcome. Beaufort is bewitched by a pretty face but finds that his perceptions can prove dangerously false; as his 'Laetitia' goes through a series of metamorphoses, he impulsively overreacts, being by turns lecherous, snobbish and nastily vindictive. The reunion of the estranged Lord and Lady Frampul reveals for each of them a past spent trying to accommodate an awareness of loss in consequence of a waning of affection. Pru's fortunes intimate that worth is not to be judged as attendant on questions of birth or breeding which are accidents of nature. The last act is at once an admission and a kind of ritual exorcism of all those elements of chance that set the permanence of felicity continually at risk. Jonson gives us the ending we crave while showing us *why* we yearn for it so assiduously, despite our suspicion of its verisilimitude. All that has diverted us throughout *The New Inn* – the games with illusion, the sport, the role-play (from the crass efforts of Pinacia to the sophisticated intellectual stances of Lovel) – are illustrations of the manifold ways by which humanity strives to accommodate itself to the depradations of chance and mutability. The characters provoke our laughter but, laughing, we understand their metaphysical dilemma. *The New Inn* shows Jonson at his most compassionate; it is also his most penetrating exploration of the nature of Comedy and of an audience's relation to that dramatic genre. Like all Jonson's best plays, it ends by profoundly enriching our long-term appreciation of the art that is theatre in performance.

The *Oxford English Dictionary* states that, though the verb, to *act*, had acquired the meanings 'to carry out in mimic action' and 'to perform on the stage' by the 1590s, it was not until nearly a century later (1684) that it took in common usuage the significance 'to perform on the stage of existence', 'to comport or demean oneself'. While Jonson never actually deployed the word in this sense, the *experience* of his plays in performance increasingly confronted his audiences with this conception of the ubiquitous presence of acting within human affairs: acting, that is, as more than a ludic pursuit. The view expressed by Jacques in *As You Like It* (II. vii.) that 'All the world's a stage / And all the men and women merely players' is, of course, something of a commonplace in Renaissance drama and poetry. Jonson, however, took the circumstance of acting before an audience and, over the space of his career, turned it into an increasingly intricate metaphysical conceit, rich in its range and precision of reference, both social and intimate. (Donne was a close friend of his.) To do this required him to keep an audience continually mindful of their relation to the stage *as an audience*. The old device of the play-within-the-play acquired at his hands a new, brilliant and subtle inventiveness. Play-situations abound in the comedies with characters assuming the functions (consciously or unconsciously) of actor, spectator, deviser, director; yet, far from being mannered or artificial, the effect of this is always to give a greater immediacy to the substance of each work by breaking down the barrier between stage and audience. The result is an experience of theatre that is exciting because combative, teasing, subversive, witty, dangerous. Jonson never flattered audiences (the Latin epigraph from Horace on the title-page of the printed text of *Bartholomew Fair* cheekily questions whether they are not all 'deaf donkeys'), yet the cunning strategies that shape his plays would seem to assume spectators whose intelligences are informed, alert and flexible, enjoying the stimulus of challenge. The history of the comedies in performance over the last thirty years shows that the most successful productions have been those that respected this appeal, and did so by exploiting to the full the flamboyant, meta-theatrical dimensions in Jonson's art. But the list of revivals is short; its brevity is a measure of our cultural loss.

Notes

1. On Inductions

1. Lionel Abel, *Metatheatre: A New View of Dramatic Form* (New York: Hill & Wang, 1963). The following quotations are from pp. 60 and 58 respectively.

2. Elizabethan Jonson

1. The bibliography describes in detail difficulties concerning accessibility of texts for some of Jonson's plays. The text of *The Case Is Altered* used here is that published in Volume Two of the Everyman Library Edition of *Ben Jonson's Plays* (London and New York: Dent, 1910; last reprinted, 1966). As this edition does not give line numbers, references are to act, scene and *page*.

2. See C. H. Herford and P. and E. Simpson (eds), *The Works of Ben Jonson* (Oxford, 1925–52), vol. XI, p. 370.

3. See I. i. pp. 666–7 and II. iv. p. 686. Anne Barton discusses these passages in *Ben Jonson, Dramatist* (Cambridge, 1984), pp. 31–2.

4. For references to *Everyman Out Of His Humour* see the text published in Volume One of the Everyman Library Edition; again act, scene and page number are given.

5. The fullest and certainly the most persuasive defence of Jonson's authorship of the additions to Kyd's *The Spanish Tragedy* is to be found in Anne Barton's *Ben Jonson, Dramatist*, pp. 13–28.

6. The texts used for the two satirical comedies, *Cynthia's Revels* and *The Poetaster*, are those printed in Volume One of the Everyman Library Edition.

7. *Every Man In His Humour* exists in two versions, one in an Italianate setting, the other situated in London. The second version, included in Jonson's *Folio* of 1616, was extensively revised throughout. Reference here is chiefly to the revised 'English' version in the text edited

by Martin Seymour-Smith for the New Mermaid Series (London, 1966; reprinted 1979). Both versions of the play are to be found in Volume One of the Everyman Library Edition; references here to the 'Italian' version, originally published in a Quarto of 1601, are to the Everyman text (pp. 1–58).

8. Relevant discussion of the Sumptuary Laws and useful quotation from them can be read in Lisa Jardine, *Still Harping On Daughters* (Brighton, 1983), pp. 141–68. *The Gentleman's Academie* or the Booke of S. Albans 'containing three most exact and excellent bookes; the first of hawking, the second of all the proper termes of hunting, and the last of armorie' was originally compiled by Iuliana Barnes in 1486; it was 'reduced into a better method' and published as a Quarto by Gervase Markham in 1595. Sir Philip Sidney's sonnet sequence, *Astrophel and Stella*, was first published in 1591; Sir Thomas Hoby's much praised translation of Castiglione's *The Book of the Courtier* appeared in 1561.

9. Charles Dickens to Miss Macready on 9 February 1845. Cited in Edgar Jonson, *Charles Dickens: His Tragedy and Triumph* (New York: Simon & Schuster, 1952), Volume One, p. 570.

10. It is now in the library of the Victoria and Albert Museum, London; Cat. no. F.33.D.8. The text used was basically Garrick's version of 1751, though, interestingly, Dickens chose to reintroduce many of Jonson's earthier expressions and sequences of dialogue that Garrick had excised. Forster, however, played the expanded number of scenes for Kitely which Garrick had devised once he had decided to play the role of the jealous husband himself.

11. Cited in Edgar Johnson, *Charles Dickens: His Tragedy and Triumph*. Both quotations appear on p. 571 of Volume One.

12. The acting text of this production of *Everyman In His Humour* was published as a programme/text with commentary by Simon Trussler by Methuen in its series *Swan Theatre Plays* in 1986.

13. See Seymour-Smith's edition of the play, cited in note 7 above, p. xxv.

3. A First Interlude: 'Sejanus His Fall'

1. See Anne Righter (Barton), *Shakespeare and the Idea of the Play*, (London, 1962).

2. *Julius Caesar*, III. i. p. 112–14. Reference is to the text published in *The Complete Oxford Shakespeare*, edited by Stanley Wells and Gary Taylor (Oxford and London, 1987).

3. References throughout this chapter to *Sejanus* relate to the text edited by W. F. Boulton for The New Mermaids Series (London, 1966).

4. Jonson took his details of the sinister omens observed in Rome and the odd behaviour of the statue of Fortune from the *Roman History* of Dio Cassius (LVIII, 5–7). Compare Shakespeare's *Julius Caesar* I. iii. and II. ii.

4. 'Volpone'

1. All references to *Volpone* relate to the text edited by Michael Jamieson in *Three Comedies: Ben Jonson* for the Penguin English Library (Harmondsworth, 1966; reprinted in Penguin Classics, 1985).

2. Ben Jonson, *Volpone*, edited by John Creaser (London, 1978), p. 23.

3. John Dennis in a letter to Congreve of 1695, cited in R. G. Noyes, *Ben Jonson on the English Stage: 1660–1776* (Harvard, Cambridge, Mass., 1935, reissued New York and London: Benjamin Blom, 1966), p. 52.

4. John Creaser in the introduction to his edition of *Volpone* for Hodder & Stoughton cited in note 2 above and Anne Barton throughout *Ben Jonson, Dramatist.*

5. The promptbooks of the two Stratford productions referred to here can be studied in the library of the Shakespeare Centre, Stratford-on-Avon; those for the National Theatre productions are kept in the archives of the Script Department at the theatre. A fuller discussion of several of the performances can be found in Arnold P. Hinchliffe, *'Volpone': Text and Performance* (Basingstoke and London, 1985) to which I am indebted for the account of Wolfit's portrayal.

5. 'Epicoene'

1. Ben Jonson, *Epicoene or The Silent Woman*, edited by L. A. Beaurline, Regents Renaissance Drama Series (London, 1966), pp. xii–xiii. All references to the play in this chapter relate to this edition.

2. Sir Thomas Overbury, *Miscellaneous Works in Prose and Verse*, edited by E. F. Rimbault (London, 1890), pp. 48 and 73 respectively.

3. See Reavley Gair, *The Children of Paul's* (Cambridge, 1982). Jonson was himself imprisoned in 1605 for his collaboration with Chapman and Marston over *Eastward Ho!*, a city comedy devised for the boys of Blackfriars that mocked the king and his Scottish associates.

4. See Ben Jonson, *The Alchemist*, edited by F. H. Mares, The Revels Plays (London, 1967), p. 4.

5. Cited in R. G. Noyes, *Ben Jonson on the English Stage: 1660–1776*, p. 187.

6. Ben Jonson, *Discoveries (1641) and Conversations with William Drummond of Hawthornden (1619)*, edited by G. B. Harrison, The Bodley Head Quartos V (London, 1923) p. 28.

7. Cited in R. G. Noyes, *Ben Jonson on the English Stage: 1660–1776*, p. 177.

8. George Colman's adaptation of the comedy was first staged by Garrick at Drury Lane on 13 January 1776, with Mrs Siddons as Epicoene.

6. 'The Alchemist'

1. All references to *The Alchemist* relate to the text edited by Michael Jamieson in *Three Comedies: Ben Jonson* for the Penguin English Library (Harmondsworth, 1966; reprinted in Penguin Classics, 1985).

2. See F. H. Mares's edition of the play in The Revels Plays Series (London, 1967), p. 4. Lady Mary was niece to Sir Philip Sidney; she wedded Sir Robert Wroth in 1604, a marriage Jonson deemed unworthy since he proved a jealous husband. Epigrammes CIII and CV and Poem XXVIII of *The Under-wood* were composed by Jonson in her praise and honour.

3. For a full discussion of crime and punishment in Elizabethan and Jacobean society see Gamini Salgado, *The Elizabethan Underworld* (New Jersey: Rowman and Littlefield, 1977).

4. Peter Womack: *Ben Jonson*, Rereading Literature Series (Oxford, 1986), pp. 117–18.

7. 'Bartholomew Fair'

1. All references to *Bartholomew Fair* relate to the text edited by Michael Jamieson in *Three Comedies: Ben Jonson* for the Penguin English Library (Harmondsworth, 1966; reprinted in Penguin Classics, 1985). I have throughout this chapter observed Jamieson's modernisation of Jonson's spelling, as currently do most editors and commentators, but it is worth pointing out that the title page of the first edition of 1631 has *Bartholmew*. The spellings, especially of names, in the 1631 text seem devised as guides to demotic pronunciation.

2. Cited in R. G. Noyes, *Ben Jonson on the English Stage: 1660–1776*, p. 244.

3. This was particularly the case with Terry Hands's revival of the play for the Royal Shakespeare Company at the Aldwych Theatre in 1969; the confusion was aggravated by a decision to dress the characters with reference to a diverse range of periods. The whole approach was cerebral in the wrong kind of way. Michael Bogdanov at the Young Vic in 1978 clearly saw the play as an excuse for his company to demonstrate their versatility in all forms of fairground and circus-style entertainment; their energetic expertise continually relegated Jonson's text to the background of an audience's awareness. Thelma Holt's production at the Roundhouse the same year achieved a powerful sense of place, raucous, sweaty and brimming with livestock, but paid little attention to the intellectual shape of the play; in consequence performances seemed oddly *flat* because of a lack of variety of tempo and tone. It was all too strenuous for climactic episodes to carry due significance. Peter Barnes's production for the Open Air Theatre in Regent's Park in 1987 had tremendous vigour but it was matched with considerable scruple, most notable in the careful orchestration of the acts and the attention paid to the time-scale of the play. The production used the open-air setting to great advantage without losing any of the intimacy essential for many of the scenes. Barnes saw the play as demanding ensemble playing of a high order, at once inventive yet selfless. This was a strength in Richard Eyre's production for the National Theatre in 1988: he presented the Fair as a child's paradise of twinkling lights and whirling carousels (the play was transposed into the late Victorian period) that tempts the starchy citizens to adopt a childish

recklessness and irresponsibility that steadily give place to total abandon. The shift into deeper levels of humour was meticulously effected. (A more detailed review of the production by the present writer can be found in the *Times Higher Education Supplement*, 9 December 1988, No. 840, p. 16.)

4. *Troilus and Cressida*, IV. vi. Also see the discussion of the similar scene in *The Staple Of News*, page 149, and of the shock-effect occasioned by Pru's insistence that Lady Frampul publicly kiss Lovel in *The New Inn*, II. vi.

5. An excellence in both Barnes's and Eyre's productions was the achievement of this subtle transition.

8. 'The Devil Is An Ass'

1. All references are to the text of *The Devil Is An Ass* edited by Gamini Salgado and published in *Four Jacobean City Comedies*, Penguin Classics (Harmondsworth, 1975; reprinted 1985).

2. Anne Barton, *Ben Jonson, Dramatist* (Cambridge, 1984), p. 219.

3. See pages 9–15.

4. William Gifford first asserted this view in his 1816 edition of the play; it has been the subject of some dispute since; Anne Barton summons forceful evidence in Gifford's defence in *Ben Jonson, Dramatist*, pp. 228 and 357–8.

5. Sadly the play has achieved only one notable revival of late and that used an adapted text by Peter Barnes. It was staged at the Birmingham Rep. and subsequently for a few performances at the Lyttleton Theatre in 1977. Its allusiveness does pose problems for modern directors but they are not insurmountable. The policy of the RSC with the Swan Theatre in staging lesser known works of the Renaissance stage should in time create the taste by which *The Devil Is An Ass* might be enjoyed.

9. A Second Interlude: the Court Masques

1. All references are to the texts of the Masques published in Stephen Orgel and Roy Strong, *Inigo Jones: The Theatre of the Stuart Court*, 2 vols (London and Berkeley/Los Angeles: Sotheby Parke Bernet and the University of California Press, 1973).

2. Stephen Orgel, *The Illusion of Power: Political Theater in the English Renaissance* (Berkeley and Los Angeles: The University of California Press, 1975).

10. Caroline Jonson

1. Anne Barton, *Ben Jonson, Dramatist* (Cambridge, 1984), pp. 300–20.

2. Lickfinger, the cook and parcel-poet, in *The Staple of News* is given many of the Cook's lines from the cancelled anti-masque to *Neptune's Triumph*, for example; the scene in that comedy where the crowd of gullible and all too credulous visitors to the Staple are sold absurdities as items of momentous news carries echoes of the anti-masque to *News*

From The New World, while the Jeerers' concept of satire is akin to that voiced by the characters designated the Curious as they adore the Satyr in *Time Vindicated to Himself and to His Honours*.

3. All references for *The Sad Shepherd* are to the text published in Volume Two of the Everyman Library Edition of *Ben Jonson's Plays* (London and New York: Dent, 1910; last reprinted, 1966). Act, scene and page references are given.

4. Inigo Jones designed a number of settings akin to this in the 1630s. See, for example, the varying prospects devised for the numerous acts of Walter Montague's pastoral play, *The Shepherd's Paradise* (Orgel and Strong, *Inigo Jones: The Theatre of the Stuart Court*, Vol. II, pp. 504–21); for *Florimene* (ibid, pp. 646–57); the Giant's Castle scene of *Britannia Triumphans* (ibid, p. 676); or the second scene, 'a peaceful country', of *Salmacida Spolia* (ibid, pp. 744–5).

5. All references are to the text of *The Staple of News* edited by Devra Rowland Kifer for the Regents Renaissance Drama Series (London, 1976).

6. See Chapter 7, page 104.

7. See III. ii. 241–8 and III. iv. 45–68.

8. All references for *The Magnetic Lady* are to the text published in Volume Two of the Everyman Library Edition of *Ben Jonson's Plays*. Act, scene and page references are given.

9. All references for *A Tale Of A Tub* are to the text published in Volume Two of the Everyman Edition of *Ben Jonson's Plays*. Act, scene and page references are given.

10. All references for *The New Inn* are to the edition by Michael Hattaway published in The Revels Plays Series (Manchester and Dover, New Hampshire: Manchester University Press, 1984).

11. The Royal Shakespeare Company staged the play in the Swan Theatre late in 1987; Fiona Shaw played Frances and John Carlisle was Lovel.

Bibliography

TEXTS OF JONSON'S PLAYS

A problem facing the serious student of Jonson's work is the current lack of a readily accessible, reasonably priced, sound edition of the Complete Plays. The standard text is *Ben Jonson* edited by C. H. Herford and Percy and Evelyn Simpson, eleven volumes (Oxford, 1925–52); but this is now out of print, not always available in libraries and organised in a fashion likely despite the excellence of its scholarship to madden all but the carefully initiated. The two-volume Everyman Library Edition of *Ben Jonson's Plays* (London and New York, 1910; last reprinted, 1966), though now out of print, is accessible in most libraries; the editing is not, however, of the soundest. The four-volume edition of the *Complete Plays* by G. A. Wilkes (Oxford, 1981–2) has made little impact on libraries. Several series of Renaissance drama texts include examples of Jonson's work, the New Mermaids (Ernest Benn), the Revels Plays (Manchester University Press), Penguin Classics, Regents Renaissance Drama (University of Nebraska Press and Edward Arnold), the Yale Ben Jonson; but none yet offers a complete run of the plays in the manner of the Arden Shakespeare. The major Jacobean comedies are available in consequence in a wealth of good editions but there are no single editions of most of Jonson's early Elizabethan comedies or of several of his late Caroline plays. As it is the policy of this series to work, where possible, with readily accessible texts, I have had to suggest particular editions for each of the plays under study rather than one specific collected edition. The notes give bibliographical details of the edition being used as each play is introduced into the discussion. A whole spectrum of editions has, however, been consulted in preparing this volume.

SELECT BIBLIOGRAPHY OF CRITICISM AND THEATRE HISTORY

(Place of publication is London except where otherwise indicated)

Barish, Jonas, *Ben Jonson and the Language of Prose Comedy* (Cambridge, Mass.: Harvard University Press, 1960)

Barton, Anne, *Shakespeare and the Idea of the Play* (Chatto & Windus, 1962)

——, *Ben Jonson, Dramatist* (Cambridge: Cambridge University Press, 1984)

Bentley, G. E., *The Jacobean and Caroline Stage*, 7 Vols (Oxford: Oxford University Press, 1941–68)

——, *The Professions of Dramatist and Player in Shakespeare's Time, 1590–1642* (New Jersey and Guildford, Princeton University Press, 1986)

Bradbrook, M. C., *The Growth and Structure of Elizabethan Comedy* (Chatto & Windus, 1955)

——, *The Rise of the Common Player* (Chatto & Windus, 1962)

Chambers, E. K., *The Elizabethan Stage*, 4 vols (Oxford: Oxford University Press, 1923)

Chan, Mary E., *Music in the Theatre of Ben Jonson* (Oxford: Clarendon Press, 1980)

Ellis-Fermor, Una, *The Jacobean Drama* (Methuen, 1936)

Gair, W. R., *The Children of Paul's: The Story of a Theatre Company, 1553–1608* (Cambridge: Cambridge University Press, 1982)

Gibbons, Brian, *Jacobean City Comedy*, Revised edition (Methuen, 1980)

Gordon, D. J., 'Poet and Architect: The Intellectual Setting of the Quarrel between Ben Jonson and Inigo Jones', *Journal of the Warburg and Courtauld Institutes*, XII (1949) pp. 152 ff

Gurr, Andrew, *The Shakespearean Stage: 1574–1642* (Cambridge: Cambridge Univesity Press, 1970)

——, *Playgoing in Shakespeare's London* (Cambridge: Cambridge University Press, 1987)

Hillebrand, H. N., *The Child Actors* (Urbana, Illinois: University of Illinois Press, 1926)

Hinchliffe, Arnold P., *'Volpone': Text and Performance* (Basingstoke: Macmillan, 1985)

Knights, L. C., *Drama and Society in the Age of Jonson* (Chatto & Windus, 1937)

Leggatt, Alexander, *Citizen Comedy in the Age of Shakespeare* (Toronto: University of Toronto Press, 1973)

Noyes, R. G., *Ben Jonson on the English Stage: 1660–1776* (Cambridge, Mass.: Harvard University Press, 1935; reissued in New York: Benjamin Blom, 1963)

Orgel, Stephen, *The Illusion of Power: Political Theater in the English Renaissance* (Berkeley, Loss Angeles: University of California Press, 1975)

—— and Strong, Roy, *Inigo Jones: The Theatre of the Stuart Court*, 2 vols (London and Berkeley, Los Angeles: Sotheby Parke Bernet and the University of California Press, 1973)

Partridge, Edward B., *The Broken Compass: A Study of the Major Comedies of Ben Jonson* (Chatto & Windus, 1958)

Salgado, Gamini, *The Elizabethan Underworld* (New Jersey: Rowman & Littlefield; London: J. M. Dent, 1977)

Strong, Roy, *Splendor at Court: Renaissance Spectacle and the Theater of Power* (Boston, Mass.: Houghton Mifflin, 1973)

Sturgess, Keith, *Jacobean Private Theatre* (Routledge & Kegan Paul, 1987)

Thomson, Peter, *Shakespeare's Theatre* (Routledge & Kegan Paul, 1983)

Wilson, Jean, *Entertainments for Elizabeth I* (Woodbridge and Totowa, New Jersey: D. S. Brewer and Rowman & Littlefield, 1980)

Womack, Peter, *Ben Jonson* (Oxford: Basil Blackwell, 1986)

Index

181